REFERENCE

W9-BYD-172

CULTURES OF THE WORLD

GERMANY

Barbara Fuller

MARSHALL CAVENDISH
New York • London • Sydney

Reference edition published 1994 by
Marshall Cavendish Corporation
2415 Jerusalem Avenue
P.O. Box 587
North Bellmore
New York 11710

© Times Editions Pte Ltd 1993

Originated and designed by
Times Books International, an imprint of
Times Editions Pte Ltd

Printed in Singapore

Library of Congress Cataloging-in-Publication Data:
Fuller, Barbara, 1961–
    Germany / Barbara Fuller.
      p. cm.—(Cultures Of The World)
    Includes bibliographical references and index.
    Summary: Explores the geography, history,
government, economy, people and culture of
Germany.
      ISBN 1-85435-530-9 (vol.):   —ISBN 1-85435-529-5 (set)
    1. Germany—Juvenile literature. [1. Germany.] I. Title.
II. Series.
DD17.F85 1992
943—dc20   92–13447
                        CIP
                        AC

Cultures of the World

Editorial Director	Shirley Hew
Managing Editor	Shova Loh
Editors	Tan Kok Eng
	Leonard Lau
	Siow Peng Han
	Sue Sismondo
	MaryLee Knowlton
Picture Editor	Yee May Kaung
Production	Edmund Lam
Design	Tuck Loong
	Ang Siew Lian
	Ong Su Ping
Illustrators	Lo Chuan Ming
	Kelvin Sim
MCC Editorial Director	Evelyn M. Fazio

INTRODUCTION

GERMANY sits in the very center of Europe, covering an area of 137,852 square miles from the North and Baltic seas in the north to the Alps in the south. Its northernmost point stretches toward Denmark; its southernmost border fronts Austria and Switzerland. To the west sit the Netherlands, Belgium and Luxembourg, with France farther south; to the east lies Poland and Czechoslovakia.

As well as being in the center of Europe, Germany's rich culture is an essential part of European and Western culture. Beethoven, Goethe, Freud, Marx—these and many such people have influenced generations of musicians, writers, philosophers and political thinkers throughout the world.

The reunification of Germany, formalized on October 3, 1990, after 45 years of separation, affects every aspect of life in the country today, from government and law enforcement to working conditions and the economy; from housing conditions and education systems to funding of the arts and sports.

All Germans share a common language and historical tradition, but local loyalties and customs often override national concerns. This book, part of the series, *Cultures of the World*, sets out to explore both the national and the local aspects of German lifestyles today.

CONTENTS

Mural paintings on a building in the town of Oberammergau.

CONTENTS

A man playing the hurdy-gurdy.

GEOGRAPHY

DURING THE LAST ICE AGE, glaciers from the Alps in the south and Scandinavia in the north advanced four times and shaped much of the land of what is now Germany. As a result, the country can be divided into three topographical areas: the North German Lowlands, the Central Uplands, and the Alps and Alpine Foreland.

The geological characteristics of each region actually cover an area farther east and west than today's frontiers. The Lowlands, for example, stretch west into the Netherlands and Belgium and east through Poland's Silesian plain to as far as the Ural Mountains in Russia. In the south, the Alps provide a natural barrier with Switzerland, and the Rhine River in the south and southwest also forms a natural border.

Opposite: **The 13th-century cathedral in the town of Limburg at dusk.**

Left: **Cattle on a Bavarian farm.**

A popular beach for vacationers on the Baltic Sea coast.

NORTH GERMAN LOWLANDS

The North Sea coast is Germany's most important shipping outlet. Along the coast are shallow tidal mud flats and dikes built to prevent flooding. Off the coast are several islands including the East Frisian Islands and Heligoland, the summit of a submerged mountain. Hamburg on the Elbe River and Bremen on the Weser are Germany's major ports, while smaller ones like Wilhelmshaven and Emden on the North Sea coast are also important.

The Baltic coast is a mixture of flat sandy shores and steep cliffs, with shallow natural inlets for ports. In the northernmost part of the country, the important Kiel Canal links the Baltic to the North Sea. The marshland near the mouth of the Elbe is fertile, but farther inland it becomes sandy, with boulders, heath, peat bogs, fens, and marshes. This infertile plain includes two major cities, Hanover and Brunswick.

South of the Baltic, a fertile belt runs from Holstein to Mecklenburg. Brandenburg's low lying plains alternate with wide marshy valleys, and because of the high water table, the houses there are built on stilts.

CENTRAL UPLANDS

The Central Uplands are the remains of old fold mountains, divided into high plains, undulating hills, mountain ranges, and wide river courses.

In the northwest, bisected by the Rhine River, are Germany's largest slate mountains—the Rhineland Schiefergebirge. These mountains in turn are separated into the Eifel Range of 50 cone-shaped extinct volcanoes; the exposed stony plateau of the Hunsrück; the agricultural areas of Sauerland and Bergischerland; the Rothaargebirge Range; the Westerwald; and the heavily-wooded Taunus region, bordered by the Main River.

Strange sandstone rock formations in the Elbe Valley near Dresden.

To the east of the Rhine and north of the Schiefergebirge is the Ruhr industrial area, where natural iron ore and hard coal deposits have led to the development of huge steel industries.

East of the Rhineland lies the Hesse Central Upland, which includes the Vogelsberg Range. To the north of these mountains is the Harz Range, source of several rivers and the site of numerous reservoirs. The east and south slopes of the Harz descend into the Thuringian Basin, where the town of Halle sits on a salt deposit. The basin is an extremely fertile region; grains and root crops are grown in the flat areas, while orchards and vineyards are found on slopes overlooking the Ilm River. Also situated in the basin is the Rennsteig, a 100-mile long footpath through the Thuringian Mountains; the Thuringian Forest, which boasts a toy-making cottage industry; and the Franconian Forest, which has slate quarries and an artificial lake.

South of the Thuringian Basin is the Erzgebirge Range, which is a natural border with Czechoslovakia. The city of Dresden sits on the plain beneath these mountains.

The breathtaking Lake Titisee in the Black Forest.

THE SOUTHERN UPLANDS South of the Schiefergebirge lies the wide Rhine flood plain, which benefits from a very favorable climate and is extremely fertile. The western hills from Frankfurt to Heidelberg are planted with fruit orchards. The Neckar Valley next to this has areas for agriculture and industry. Two of the world's most famous forests lie to the south of the Central Uplands—the Black Forest in the southwest and the Bavarian Forest in the southeast. The Black Forest, which got its name from its extensive dark fir trees, is the source of the Danube and Neckar rivers. The Bavarian Forest, experiencing a booming tourism trade because of its national park, is mainly covered with coniferous trees.

ALPS AND PRE-ALPS

The Danube, rising in the Black Forest and leaving Germany at Passau in the east on its way to the Black Sea, runs along the northern edge of the Alpine Foreland, which rises to an average height of 1,640 feet. Among the rounded hills are some popular lakes—the Chiemsee, Starnbergersee, and Ammersee, to name a few.

The northern part of the region, Lower Bavaria, has very fertile soil where hops is grown for the breweries in nearby Munich. It also has bogs where the water table is high. The southern part of the region is higher and wetter, suitable for raising cattle. Augsburg and Munich are the main population centers of the region.

Fir trees with the German Alps in the background.

In the southwest, Lake Constance—37 miles long and nine miles wide—is nestled in the depression of alpine fallout moraines. Together with the Chiemsee, Lake Constance makes up part of the Alpine lakes, the focus of considerable settlement, a booming tourism industry, and scientific studies. The island of Mainau on the lake has a unique climate.

To the east of Lake Constance, at the frontier with Austria, are the German Alps. From west to east, these are divided into the Allgäu, the Bavarian, and the Berchtesgaden Alps. The north-facing alpine slopes are forested, while farms with pasture lands dot the south-facing slopes. The lower slopes below 3,000 feet have mixed forests, conifers lie between 3,000 feet and the tree line at 5,600 feet, while there is year-round snow at over 8,500 feet.

The Zugspitze ("ZOOG-spits-er"), at 9,725 feet, is Germany's highest mountain, while nearby Garmisch-Partenkirchen, the largest town in the Bavarian Alps, is Germany's major ski resort.

A barge on the Rhine River near Düsseldorf.

THE RHINE

The Rhine River is 820 miles long, the second longest in Europe and one of the most famous. It comes from the Alps in the south and flows to the North Sea, forming a natural border between Germany and Switzerland from Lake Constance to the Swiss town of Basel, and between France and Germany from Basel to near Karlsruhe. Along its banks are breathtaking vineyards, fortresses, castles, and picturesque towns.

For 552 miles, the river is navigable—it is the busiest waterway in Europe, with 9,000 cargo vessels using it each month. In the Alps and Alpine Foreland, the river moves rapidly, turning into spectacular waterfalls at Schaffhausen in Switzerland. It then opens onto a wide plateau from Karlsruhe to Mainz, where a wide variety of crops are grown along its banks. North of Mainz, the river plunges into a gorge through the Schiefergebirge before opening out once more into a wider flood plain to the north of Koblenz. Between Cologne and the border with the Netherlands, the Rhine flows through the large Ruhr industrial area.

EAST AND WEST

The division of Germany into East—the Deutsche Demokratische Republik ("DOY-cher Demm-oh-CRATT-ish-er Rep-oo-BLEEK")—and West—the Bundesrepublik Deutschland ("BOON-dess Rep-oo-BLEEK DOY-chs-lant")—between 1945 and 1990 affected every part of German life and geography. Even today, it is still in a phase of rapid change.

Agricultural development, landholding patterns, industrial practice, housing stock, and forms of law enforcement and government all differed greatly from East to West.

Environmental concerns about industrial pollution, long overdue efforts to preserve historical buildings, maintaining housing in adequate condition, and restoring land seized by the former East German state from families are just some of the issues the newly reunited country has to resolve and finance. Together with the very visible contrasts between the two former states, social and economic problems are arising with different attitudes toward work, wealth, hopes, and standards of living.

The Neuschwanstein Castle in Bavaria looks like something from Disneyland. It was built by King Ludwig II of Bavaria in the 1870s.

13

THE BERLIN WALL

The postwar Russian zone, which became East Germany, had suffered some of the worst wartime bomb damage as well as extremely demanding postwar compensation payments. It experienced an almost immediate population drain to West Germany after World War II.

During the early 1950s, the border between the two states was guarded by watch towers and barbed wire from the Eastern side, but a steady stream of emigrants, totalling about 3.5 million, continued to leave through Berlin. However, on August 12, 1961, an 11-foot high concrete wall was constructed overnight, dividing the communist East from the West. The wall quickly became a symbol of the oppression of the East German regime, turning the former capital into a divided city as the main street—Unter den Linten—was blocked by part of the 40-mile barrier. At least 72 people lost their lives attempting to cross the wall, 55 of whom were shot to death by East German security forces. The last victim, Chris Gueffroy, was shot in February 1989, and the four border guards responsible for his death are today serving prison sentences for manslaughter.

In the late 1980s, popular unrest and protests began, ending in the fall of the communist government and the opening of the wall on November 9, 1989. When that happened, a flood of Germans from both East and West streamed through. Pieces of the wall have now become popular souvenirs, and the monument itself has even become a sunbathing spot.

STATES

Before reunification, there were 10 states in the Federal Republic of Germany (West Germany). These remain in today's united country. From north to south, they are Schleswig-Holstein, with Kiel as its capital; Lower Saxony, with Hanover; North Rhine-Westphalia, with Düsseldorf; Hesse, with Wiesbaden; Rhineland-Palatinate, with Mainz; Saarland, with Saarbrücken; Baden-Württemberg, with Stuttgart; Bavaria, with Munich; and the city states of Hamburg and Bremen. West Berlin was the 11th state, but with a different legal status, still technically administered and defended by the World War II victors France, Britain, and the United States.

The former East German states of Mecklenburg-Vorpommern, Brandenburg, Saxony, Thuringia, and Saxony-Anhalt were turned into 14 different administrative districts. Since reunification, these districts have gone back to their original statehoods, and East and West Berlin have been joined into a single new city state. Today, each of Germany's 16 states has its own elected parliament and local government structure.

An interesting sculpture at the City Center in Berlin. In the distance is the Memorial Church, which was badly damaged during World War II.

CITIES

There is no single dominant city in Germany, which has a strong tradition of local self-government. Wealth, industry, and cultural activities are spread around the whole country, and this prevents a common problem of overconcentration of resources in one area at the expense of others.

BERLIN The former divided city is now an artistic and cultural center, with over 200 musical groups, an annual jazz festival, alternative modern artists and fringe theaters, left-wing thinkers, and radical supporters of the peace movement. Berlin has a large gay community. It also has the largest Turkish population of any city outside Turkey.

The Kurfürstendamm is a two-mile long street in the amusement and shopping district of the city where shops stay open very late. In June 1991, Germany voted to return its capital to Berlin, with the Bundestag (the national parliament) transferring there within 10 years.

MUNICH A cultural and intellectual city, it is also a fashion capital and a world-renowned brewing center. The city center is only one mile across, and no skyscrapers are allowed to interrupt the original style of architecture. Munich hosted the 1972 Olympics, so its sports and leisure facilities are excellent, as is its transportation system. Siemens, BMW, and MBB Aerospace are all based in Munich, as well as a host of electronics and advanced technology companies.

STUTTGART Set in a picturesque hollow of terraced suburbs surrounded by vineyards and forested hills, Stuttgart feels small despite its surrounding industrial area which contains major companies like Bosch, Daimler Benz, Porsche, Standard Electric Lorenz, and German IBM. The downtown area is quite new, having been rebuilt after World War II. Stuttgart has a famous ballet troupe, several foreign consulates, and inviting open air cafés along the Schlossplatz, the central pedestrian zone.

FRANKFURT-AM-MAIN The city has been a banking center since the 16th century. The Stock Exchange of Germany and headquarters of most German banks are located in the city center. Frankfurt's level of commerce supports a big budget for spending on the arts, architecture, and conservation. It is also a publishing center, hosting an annual international book fair each October. Frankfurt is an international and metropolitan town, with a bright intellectual life. Twenty-two percent of its population are immigrant workers.

Lovely red flowers line a park in Stuttgart.

The evening sun gives Cologne a golden look.

BONN This old university town—where classical composer Ludwig van Beethoven was born—was the capital of former West Germany from 1945 to 1991. Many of its residents are university professors and students, government civil servants, and foreign diplomats. Beethoven's birthplace, the Beethovenhaus, is a museum housing instruments, scores, and memorabilia. With the decision to relocate the capital to Berlin, Bonn is preparing for a downturn in employment and economic life.

COLOGNE Cologne used to be the ancient Roman Empire's leading colony. Today, it has several Romanesque churches as well as a world-renowned cathedral. The city was badly damaged during World War II—90% of the city center was destroyed—and has a lot of unsympathetic postwar architecture. Despite this, Cologne is an open and friendly city, and its people enjoy a good local TV station, several museums, a lively art market, and a spectacular carnival. Because of its location, Cologne has become a major rail junction and important inland port.

HAMBURG The city is built on water and has 2,195 bridges over the River Elbe, Lake Alster, and many canals. The lake can freeze over during the winter. There are few skyscrapers in the city center, which has mostly red-brick architecture. The once prosperous port is now struggling to compete with Rotterdam and with the European Community tariff regulations. Hamburg has a Sunday morning fish market, which closes at 10 a.m. sharp so as not to clash with church services.

DRESDEN The site of the worst bombing during the last stages of World War II, Dresden was almost completely destroyed. However, some of its older buildings were rebuilt. Today, it has an ugly mixture of postwar structures—of which many need replacing—and a few older buildings. Under the communist regime, the buildings which survived Allied bombs fell into disrepair, and several, including the Stadtschloss that dated from 1443, were destroyed. Following reunification, unemployment and consequent unrest have resulted in growing extremist activity in the city.

At night, the lights of Dresden give the Elbe River a beautiful glow.

The town of Heidelberg at night during winter.

CLIMATE

The northwest of Germany has an Atlantic climate similar to that of the American Northwest: west winds, cool summers, moderate winters, and a high annual rainfall. Situated on an unprotected plain, it receives the full brunt of the Atlantic conditions.

In the northeast, there are bitterly cold winters, as the area receives the force of the Russian winds, with hot summers and relatively low rainfall.

The Alpine region is more Continental, with warm but short summers and cold, snowy winters. However, it has less fierce winds than those experienced in the northeast.

The best climate is found in the Rhine rift valley, which has an early spring, light rainfall, warm summers, and few frosts—the ideal climate for agriculture as well as tourism. Average January temperatures are 35 F in the lowlands and 21 F in the mountains. In the summer, the temperatures are 63 F in the mountains and 68 F in the upper Rhine valley. The driest month is February, while in the Alps the annual amount of rain is 58 inches.

FLORA AND FAUNA

Forests cover 30% of German territory, and all are open to the public. About 45% of the forests are pine, 40% beech, and 8% oak. Where there is enough light and good soil in the forests, dog's mercury, sweet woodruff, and violets grow. And at higher levels, balsam, willow herb, monkshood, bilberry, foxgloves, and wavy hair grass are found.

In 1980, the first signs of pollution were noticed when trees were found to be dying and failing to recover, probably due to acid rain caused by sulphur dioxide emissions from industry. These dying forests are one of Germany's most important ecological issues. Regulations to reduce pollution caused by cars have been introduced to try to prevent further damage.

Flowers in full bloom in the German countryside.

The government has strict anti-pollution laws, with industries facing heavy fines for discharging poisonous emissions. The Rhine River and its valley has been the target of a recent clean-up campaign, and various nature conservation groups advise using natural rather than chemical pesticides to rid the area of insects.

Some of the former border territories between the two Germanys have been turned into nature reserves. A 5,680-acre area along Lake Schaal between Schleswig-Holstein and Mecklenburg plays host to a variety of sea eagles, cranes, cormorants, bitterns, greylag geese, osprey, and other birds. Much of the Lüneburg heath region in the northeast is a nature reserve, and in Bavaria, the national park along the border with Czechoslovakia is another wildlife reserve. Wild boar and deer are hunted in Bavaria, and deer are also found in mountainous areas such as the Harz Mountains and the Alpine Foothills.

HISTORY

THE HISTORY OF GERMANY IS RELATIVELY RECENT, since the country was first united as a political nation only in 1871. But the history of the German people is much, much older.

EARLY HISTORY

During the Bronze Age, there were Germanic peoples in southern Scandinavia and northern Germany. Around the first century, the Romans attempted to expand their empire in the northeast, but were repulsed by the German Cherusci tribe under their leader Arminius in A.D. 9. After that, the Romans kept the Rhine and Danube rivers as their borders with the Germanic peoples, and reinforced these natural barriers with a 341-mile-long wall, called the Limes, parts of which can still be seen today.

The arrival of the Mongoloid Huns at the end of the 3rd century started the migrations of Germanic tribes, Ostrogoths, Visigoths, and Vandals which was known as the *Volkerwanderung* ("FOLL-ker-van-der-ung"). The Vandals crossed the Rhine River in A.D. 46, effectively bringing to an end the Roman Empire in the region. Goths and other Germanic tribes settled there, along with the Vandals, in the second half of the 4th century.

At the end of the 5th century, the neighboring Franks under the Merovingian king, Clovis, expanded political control over territories from northern Spain and the Atlantic coast to the Rhine, converting all the people to Christianity. By the beginning of the 8th century, the Franks had conquered all Germanic tribes except the Saxons.

Hohenschwangan castle in Bavaria, a medieval fortress rebuilt in the 19th century.

THE MIDDLE AGES

Charlemagne, known in German as Karl der Grosse (768–814), was crowned Holy Roman Emperor in A.D. 800. He conquered and converted the Saxons to Christianity in 805. After Charlemagne's death, the kingdom of the East Franks became the Germanic kingdom under Ludwig the German (843–876); that of the West Franks became what is now France; and the land in the middle, Lotharingia, became Lorraine.

Later, another German king, Otto I the Great (936–973), defeated the Hungarian Magyars at Lechfeld in 955, conquered northern Italy, and was crowned Holy Roman Emperor in 962. From then until 1806, all German kings became emperors. The church became an administrative part of the empire, gaining wealth, land, and importance in the mutually advantageous years of expansion.

Under Heinrich IV (1056–1106), there was a dispute with the Pope, leading to a split of the Christian Empire and to disunity among the German princes within the Germanic kingdom. Friedrich I of the Hohenstaufen Dynasty, also known as Barbarossa (1115–1190), started wars against the Pope, the Italians, and the Saxons, but the rise of the individual German dukes weakened him by the end of the Hohenstaufen Era in 1268, and the monarchy eventually became a pawn of the dukes.

Germanic colonization east of the Elbe River took place at this time, with Teutonic knights spreading Christianity along most of the Baltic coasts. In 1356, the empire set out the rules to elect a king for all of Germany, with increasingly important towns as well as the princes having votes.

THE HAPSBURG DYNASTY

The rise of the Hapsburg Dynasty saw Rudolf I (1273–1291) virtually control Germany and Austria. The next Hapsburg rulers, Maximilian I (1483–1519) and his grandson Charles V (1519–1556), were both powerful Holy Roman emperors.

It was during this dynasty, in 1517, that Martin Luther posted 95 theses on the church door at Wittenberg, to protest various abuses in the Catholic Church and set in motion the great chain of events known today as the Protestant Reformation.

Within a few years, many of the princes and dukes had become Protestant, and religious wars were fought until the Peace of Augsburg in 1555, which allowed Protestants the same rights of worship as Catholics. Roughly four-fifths of Germany became Protestant. This changed slightly after the Catholic Counter Reformation started by the Council of Trent (1545–1563), when many of the abuses Luther had protested were corrected.

Unfortunately, peace did not last for long. The Thirty Years' War (1618–1648), fueled by religious hatred, eventually ended in the Treaty of Westphalia, after Germany's population had been reduced by one-third. The peace took away much of the remaining power of the Hapsburg monarchy. It also deprived Germany of access to the sea, leaving 1,800 independent political kingdoms. Some of the rulers, including those of the two most powerful states, Frederick the Great II of Prussia and Joseph II of Austria, ruled wisely with regard to culture and philosophy.

The church door at Wittenberg, where Martin Luther posted his 95 theses.

One of Germany's greatest politicians, Otto von Bismarck.

19TH-CENTURY GERMANY

France's 1789 revolution and its effects produced ripples in neighboring Germany, but when the left bank of the Rhine River and Berlin were occupied during the Napoleonic Wars and the last Holy Roman Emperor, Franz II, was forced from the throne in 1806, the fires of German nationalism were lit.

At the Congress of Vienna in 1815 that convened at the end of the Napoleonic Wars, a German Confederation was formed—35 states and four cities, with a parliament in Frankfurt. In 1834, a German Customs Union was formed, which increasing numbers of smaller states joined, creating an inland market in place of a whole range of customs, currencies, and controls.

The northeastern state of Brandenburg-Prussia expanded its power during the second half of the 19th century under the leadership of its prime minister, Otto von Bismarck. The German-Danish War of 1864 gained Schleswig and Holstein for Prussia and Austria. In 1866, Prussia defeated Austria to secure these lands, making it the most powerful state in Germany.

Prussia subsequently dissolved the German Confederation and replaced it with the North German Federation. Bismarck was chosen chancellor of this federation, and in 1870, a short victorious war over France added the provinces of Alsace and Lorraine. The southern German states later joined their northern neighbors, forming the German Empire, or Reich ("RYE-k"). On January 18, 1871, King William I of Prussia became the Kaiser ("KYE-ser") or German emperor of an empire of 20 states and three cities.

WORLD WAR I

After a long arms race, crises in Morocco and the Balkans, and increasing competition between the different European powers, war was sparked off by the assassination of the heir to the Austrian throne in Serbia in June 1914. Austria invaded Serbia with German support, while Russia sided with Serbia, supported by France. Germany then declared war on France, invading Belgium in order to destroy French defences. This brought Great Britain into the war in defence of Belgian neutrality.

World War I was initially expected to be over by Christmas, but it became the worst war in the history of Europe. Fighting in the trenches in northeastern France dragged on for four long and painful years, with terrible casualties on both sides. Battles at Verdun and the Somme became examples of the horrors of war. The United States' entry into the war in 1917 helped turn the tide against Germany and its allies.

In November 1918, following a ceasefire, a treaty was agreed to and World War I ended. The Kaiser gave up his throne and fled.

German artillery firing at French troops during the height of the Battle of Verdun in 1916. This battle, which cost the lives of more than 600,000 German and French soldiers, was one of the most terrible in history.

RESULTS OF WORLD WAR I The Treaty of Versailles held Germany and its allies fully responsible for the war, and the victors imposed reparations (war payments) and tried to prevent a rise of the German military.

In the war and subsequent peace, Germany lost 27,000 square miles of territory, 7.2 million people, 15% of its farming output, 10% of its manufacturing capacity, 75% of its iron ore production, and all its overseas colonies. East and West Prussia were separated to allow Poland access to the Baltic Sea, and Danzig (now Gdansk in Poland) was declared a free city. Alsace-Lorraine went to France, which also occupied the Saarland industrial area. Three million Germans were left outside German territory.

From left to right: **Field Marshal Paul von Hindenburg, Kaiser Wilhelm II and General Erich Ludendorff in the German headquarters planning another assault against the Allies during World War I. Hindenburg later became the president of Germany.**

THE WEIMAR REPUBLIC

Statues on top of the Brandenburg Gate in Berlin.

Germany's first republic was an experiment with democracy soon after its devastating military defeat. Well-meaning but ultimately unconvincing Social Democrat politicians attempted to put the country back on its feet, but the loss of Alsace-Lorraine to France, and the heavy reparations burden crippled the country economically. In 1923, Germany could not pay its reparations, which led France to occupy the Ruhr coalfields to extract its own form of compensation.

Morale dropped drastically, and inflation reached terrifying proportions. One dollar was worth 9 marks in 1919. By January 1923 it was worth 17,972 marks, and by November 1923 it was worth 4.2 billion marks, vitually leading the country into a barter economy where goods were exchanged. The stock market crash of 1929 and consequent Great Depression left Germany with 7 million people unemployed. This eventually led to the rise of right-wing and left-wing extremist groups.

THE HITLER YEARS

The National Socialist movement or the Nazis, an extreme right-wing organization led by Adolf Hitler, rose in power during the depression. It opposed communism and blamed Jewish bankers and financiers, as well as France's hostile reparations demands, for Germany's plight. Its objective was to start a German nation which included all the territories and German nationals lost in 1918. Support for the Nazis grew, and by 1932 they had become the strongest party in parliament.

On January 30, 1933, Hitler was appointed chancellor by President Hindenburg. In 1934, Hindenburg died and Hitler proclaimed himself leader or Führer ("FOO-rer"). In 1935, the Saarland voted to return to Germany, and the following year Hitler remilitarized the Rhine area in spite of the Versailles peace terms. Rearmament increased manufacturing, and large-scale highway construction led to full employment. These made the Nazis popular.

Hitler's insane vision of German racial supremacy began. He favored the Aryan or white race, supported selective genetic breeding and the destruction of the Jewish race. Jews were deprived of their civil rights and Jewish businesses and synagogues were destroyed in a systematically organized form of brutality. During the 1940s, in what is known as the Final Solution, Hitler sent millions of Jews to concentration camps where most were tortured and killed.

WORLD WAR II Hitler's foreign policy aim of uniting the German people into a greater Germany which would dominate Europe began with the annexation of Austria in 1938. This caused little anxiety. However, there

A German paratrooper during World War II. The paratroopers were one of the best fighting forces in the German army. But during the invasion of Greece, they were almost wiped out by the British Army and had to be disbanded.

was more international concern when parts of Czechoslovakia were annexed. On September 1, 1939, World War II erupted when Germany invaded Poland. Britain and France immediately declared war on Germany. Poland was defeated in a month and divided between Germany and the Soviet Union, according to a secret treaty signed by the two countries.

Former Prussian lands were "returned" to Germany. Hitler then turned his armies northward and conquered Denmark and Norway, then back south to occupy Belgium, Holland, France, Yugoslavia, and Greece.

In 1940 Germany and Italy formed an alliance and the conflict spread to North Africa. In 1941 Hitler turned against his former ally, the Soviet Union, and invaded Russia. When Japan attacked Pearl Harbor in December 1941, Germany immediately declared war on the United States.

The war went well for Germany until late 1942, when its armies suffered terrible losses in the Soviet Union and North Africa. In 1943 Allied troops invaded Italy and soon the Italians surrendered. And because Germany could not defeat the United Kingdom in 1941 during the Battle of Britain,

The city of Dresden after the terrible firebombing by Allied planes in 1945.

Allied troops used the British Isles as a base, landed in France in 1944 and swept through western Europe and into Germany. From the east, Soviet armies drove non-stop all the way to Berlin. On April 30, 1945, surrounded on all sides, Hitler committed suicide and Germany surrendered.

West Germany was rapidly restored by the Allies after World War II. It joined the North Atlantic Treaty Organization in the 1950s, reforming its army in 1956. In 1963, United States president John F. Kennedy visited the country to develop close relations, and summed up his feelings during a visit to Berlin: "Ich bin ein Berliner!" (I am a Berliner.)

POSTWAR GERMANY

Immediately after its surrender, Germany was demilitarized and divided into four administrative zones by the victorious powers of France, Britain, the United States, and the Soviet Union. An agreement to govern Germany was reached between Britain, the United States, and the Soviet Union in late 1945. Königsberg (now Kaliningrad) and all of northeastern Prussia was given to the Soviet Union, while all German territories east of the Oder River were subjected to Polish administration until a final settlement was reached. This led to a large-scale emigration of 13 million Germans moving westward into today's Germany. As many as 1 million may have died on the way.

With the start of the Cold War between the East and the West, worries about German reconstruction disappeared as a new set of priorities—stopping the spread of communism—emerged in the West. In 1948, the French, American, and British zones were turned into the Federal Republic of Germany, with its own laws. The next year Konrad Adenauer was appointed its first federal chancellor. This country was regarded as a temporary solution until the eastern section joined it.

THE BERLIN AIRLIFT

In June 1948, the Soviet Union blockaded the western part of Berlin, closing all land corridors and railway access to the city from the West. The blockade lasted 10 months, from June 1948 to May 1949. The gamble failed because the West flew a total of 120,000 flights into West Berlin, bringing 1.5 million tons of food, medical supplies, and other essentials to supply the 2 million inhabitants. Eventually, Soviet leader Josef Stalin realized that he could not win the city this way, and the blockade was lifted.

The country remained occupied and only attained self rule in 1955. The eastern sector, or Russian zone, became East Germany or the Democratic Republic of Germany. East Germans came under the rule of the Socialist Unity Party (SED) or the East German Communist Party, led by Walter Ulbricht.

Within the Russian zone lay the historic capital, Berlin, itself also divided into four administrative zones. The British, American, and French zones were well run, but the Russian zone remained hostile. When West Germany introduced radical postwar currency reform in 1948, Soviet leader Josef Stalin attempted to win the whole city for the communist East by imposing a blockade.

The most famous border post in the world—Checkpoint Charlie. This was the main border opening between former East and West Berlin.

For more than 40 years, East and West Berliners dreamed of meeting each other. But they were separated by a wall that prevented crossing over from either side. In 1989, the wall came down and the dream came true.

EAST-WEST GERMAN RELATIONS

With the introduction of communist principles, the redistribution of land and wealth, and the Soviet Union's crippling reparations demands, thousands of East Germans were forced to cross to the wealthier West. Besides economic reasons, many families had been divided by the new frontier. In June 1953, an uprising in East Berlin and other East German towns was forcibly put down by Soviet troops. The 855-mile border between East and West Germany was fortified to become a closely guarded barrier, called the Iron Curtain. Then in August 1961, the Berlin Wall was built.

During the 1960s, at the height of the Cold War, there was little communication between the two Germanys. Then later that decade, Chancellor Willy Brandt of West Germany started *Ostpolitik* ("OST-poll-ee-teek"), meeting the East German government in order to help individual families. A few years later, a treaty between East and West was signed. West German citizens were gradually allowed to visit relatives in the East for limited periods, but East Germans were not allowed to travel to the West.

REUNIFICATION

The West German constitution had always regarded the division of Germany as temporary and provided for the reunification of the country. West Germany always welcomed as citizens all East German refugees who did manage the incredibly difficult passage across the border.

When Soviet leader Mikhail Gorbachev started his policy of *glasnost*, or openness, in the Soviet Union in the late 1980s, the gradual decrease of Soviet control over East Germany and Eastern Europe led to peaceful revolutions.

In May 1989, East Germans on vacation in Hungary took advantage of the country's newly opened borders and crossed via Austria into West Germany. Other East Germans sought refuge at West German embassies in Czechoslovakia and Poland. Later that year, the first steps toward reunification were taken when East German travel restrictions were lifted. A visit by Gorbachev in October 1989 made it clear that Soviet troops would no longer support the country. Barely a month later, the Berlin Wall, the symbol of division, was torn down. Talks on reunification between the East and West German governments progressed rapidly and a treaty of unification was signed on October 3, 1990.

The first full democratic parliamentary elections took place two months later and Helmut Kohl was elected as chancellor of a reunified Germany. Former East German leader Erich Honecker fled to the Soviet Union just before facing charges of ordering the deaths of East German refugees. He took refuge in the Chilean Embassy in Moscow and is suffering from cancer.

Germans chipping away at the Berlin Wall. Many people have taken parts of the wall as souvenirs.

35

GOVERNMENT

GERMANY HAS A FEDERAL, decentralized system of government, meaning each state—called Land ("LANN-t")—has total power and its own constitution within the guidelines laid down in the Basic Law, Germany's set of governing laws. This style of government has its roots in the 15th century, and allows a wide application of democratic principles on the local and national level. A number of national politicians have gained valuable experience from working at these levels.

There are many checks and balances on the central power in this system. For example, the head of the government—the federal chancellor—is only in charge of the armed forces in times of war; during peacetime, the army remains under the control of the federal minister of defense.

Opposite: **A German military standard.**

Left: **East meets West. Former East German leader Erich Honecker (left) meets Helmut Kohl, who is currently chancellor of the united Germany.**

The interior of the German parliament in Bonn.

FEDERAL GOVERNMENT

There are two houses of government: the Bundestag ("BOON-des-targ"), elected by citizens every four years, which in turn elects the federal chancellor; and the Bundesrat ("BOON-des-rart"), comprised of nominees from the state governments, which represent the interests of the different states. Voting is not compulsory, but anyone above 18 years of age has the right to vote.

The German president is the head of state, elected every five years by the federal assembly and state representatives. He officially appoints the federal chancellor once he is elected by the Bundestag.

The federal government has recently voted to move the Bundestag from its premises in Bonn to Berlin. The process is lengthy and expected to take about 10 years. The Bundesrat has voted to remain in Bonn for the time being. The federal government is responsible for defense, foreign policy, postal services, rail and air facilities, currency, trade tariffs, and issuing passports. It shares responsibility with the state governments for civil and criminal law enforcement, labor law, road traffic and economic matters, having the prior right to legislate. Income from taxes is divided between the federal and state governments.

Former West Germany became a North Atlantic Treaty Organization member in 1954, and joined the United Nations in 1973. Its army, the *Bundeswehr* ("BOON-des-ware"), is a purely defensive force. Germany requires that all men give 12 months of national service. "Conscientious objectors" (those who do not want to serve in the army for moral principles) can work in hospitals instead. In 1991 there were 90,000 conscientious objectors.

STATE GOVERNMENTS

Each of the states, or Länder, has its own elected parliament—called *Landesrat* ("LANN-des-rart"). As with the federal government, voting is optional and all citizens over 18 have the right to vote.

The state governments are responsible for health care, education policies, broadcasting, and cultural affairs. They make and administer local government laws and environmental protection measures, run their own police force, and enforce traffic regulations and federal laws.

The local governments in turn look after the local towns, communities, and counties. Mayors are well paid so as to attract talented individuals to such positions.

The local authorities collect certain taxes and share in others, though each state grants them additional revenues to keep solvent. Revenue problems frequently arise at the state level.

For instance, the city-state of Hamburg has high property taxes; those who can live just outside its borders and commute pay lower rates and this decreases the revenue Hamburg receives.

The Munich City Hall and Promenade.

The former East German states are currently heavily dependent on funds from the federal government in order to attain a standard of living comparable to the western German states. Large sums of money are needed to improve and restore housing stock, upgrade industries, and turn local economies competitive.

The current aid program to the five former East German states amounts to DM 6,100 for each inhabitant.

POLITICAL PARTIES

There are five major political parties in Germany. The Christian Democratic Union (CDU) and the Christian Social Union (CSU) from Bavaria form one parliamentary block, drawing support from Protestants and Catholics. The CDU, where Chancellor Helmut Kohl is from, is the only party to gain large-scale support in East Germany. The Social Democratic Party (SPD), the Free Democratic Party (FDP), and the Green Party make up the rest. The German Communist Party (KPD), which was banned in 1923 but resurfaced as the Socialist Unity Party (SED), was the party in power in former East Germany from 1945 to 1990.

There are various other smaller political parties, generally more powerful at the state than at the federal level. But their political power is hampered by a law that says only parties which have gain 5% or more of the votes in an election can send representatives to the Bundestag—a check which has so far stopped extreme right- and left-wing parties from gaining seats.

A sculpture in front of the German chancellor's office in Bonn.

THE LEGAL SYSTEM

Germany has a highly-regulated society, with thousands of federal and state laws as well as customary and case laws. The bulk of German law is codified and regulations govern people's lives: citizens must carry identification cards or papers, drive with their license and insurance documents, and can be fined for crossing the road where there is no pedestrian crossing.

The Basic Law's scope has been extended to carry out unification. It lays out numerous rules to protect democracy and press freedom, and guarantees a catalog of human rights well beyond the usual laws, including the granting of protection to political refugees. There is no death penalty in the country.

There are five different types of courts: the ordinary court for criminal and civil cases, the labor court for labor relations, the administrative court for all administrative laws, the social court for social programs, and the fiscal court for tax matters. The federal constitutional court is the highest court of appeal as well as a constitutional and legislative body.

The Social Democratic Party or SPD having a general meeting.

The legal system in former East Germany is one of the many complex issues being resolved at present, since all judges and magistrates as well as lawyers were trained in the highly political communist system. There is evidence that many may be guilty of maltreatment and torture of prisoners.

The state of Saxony is the first to have checked through the records of all its judges, and has confirmed 50% in their posts. This process is still under way in the remaining states.

The police force, too, is unwilling to do more than keep order until their role in the new Germany is confirmed. The former East German secret police, the *Stasi* ("STAR-zee"), kept numerous files on German citizens. However, its former members, along with roughly 5,000 former East German spies, are being brought to trial for past crimes.

Attempts are being made to extradite former East German leader Erich Honecker from Russia to face charges.

ECONOMY

GERMANY IS ONE OF THE WORLD'S leading industrial economies. It belongs to the G-7 group, which represents the seven richest nations in the world. And as a leading power in the European Community, it is working for closer economic union. Even its banks are powerful. For example, the Deutsche Bundesbank's decisions on money matters and interest rates affect all European currencies tied to the Deutschmark by the European Monetary System. Besides that, the Deutschmark is one of the yardsticks by which the American dollar is measured.

Germany's fantastic economic growth rate is experiencing a temporary decline in the 1990s, due to worldwide recession and the cost of reabsorbing the people and inefficient industries of former East Germany.

Opposite: **The magnificent BMW Tower in Munich.**

Left: **Downtown Frankfurt, the financial center of Germany.**

Workers harvesting pota-
toes in Mecklenburg.

POSTWAR ECONOMIC MIRACLE

Over half of West Germany's industrial capacity was destroyed during
World War II, and a further 5% was taken from existing capital and foreign
assets as part of war payments. In East Germany, the Soviet Union took
current production, and sometimes even entire plants, back to the USSR.
Yet during the 1950s, West Germany experienced an economic miracle,
called the *Wirtschaftswunder* ("VIRT-shafts-woon-der"). As a result, the
country reached economic stability by 1953, full employment by 1959, and
industrial production rose by 130% in the late 1950s.

A number of factors contributed to this success. The Marshall Plan,
started by the United States, injected necessary economic aid during
reconstruction. A daring currency reform made money worth working for
and attacked inflation. Price and wage controls were abolished and a
sensible industrial relations policy was achieved. Modern industrial facilities
replaced those destroyed by war, while the Korean War in the 1950s
increased demand for manufactured goods.

INFRASTRUCTURE AND COMMUNICATIONS

With the *Wirtschaftswunder*, Germany has become a highly efficient country. For example, the federal government owns and subsidizes both the postal and railway services. And even though the passenger service runs at a loss, the cargo service makes a profit.

One good thing came out of the Nazi era for Germany—a solid infrastructure of roads and highways was built. This network spreads out from Berlin to all over Germany. It expanded rapidly during former West Germany's car boom period of the 1950s, and remains a spectacular achievement. The former West Germany had 4,910 miles of highways, a network second in length only to that of the United States. Cars account for 75% of passenger traffic. There is currently no speed limit on the highways, and the influential German car lobby hopes to keep this freedom.

Germany also has an extensive network of inland waterways—rivers and canals—linking the industrial towns of the Rhine River with the Baltic ports and the rest of the European market.

For instance, 25% of manufactured and agricultural goods are transported on water, of which 70% goes through the Rhine River. The Kiel Canal across the state of Schleswig-Holstein is a busy route for goods traveling between the Baltic and North seas.

Lufthansa is the national airline and 75% of it is owned by the state. As for telecommunications and satellites, Germany has some of the most modern and efficient in the world.

A barge entering a lock in the canal at Magdeburg.

THE GERMAN CAR INDUSTRY

The German car industry is the largest in Europe. In 1985, 4 million vehicles were produced, of which 65% were sold to other countries.

The car industry in Germany is extremely powerful. It has so far lobbied successfully against any speed limits on the country's well-maintained highways.

The greatest success has been in the expensive high performance vehicles. Probably the most famous luxury car in the world today had its beginnings in Germany. A man named Gottlieb Daimler invented the gasoline engine in the 1880s in the city of Stuttgart, while another, Karl Benz, was starting similar developments some 80 miles away in Mannheim.

When they met, they decided to work together to design an automobile. The result was, in 1899, a new Daimler car, named after manager Emil Jellinek's daughter, Mercedes. Though the Daimler and Benz companies only fully merged in 1960, Mercedes Benz has been a household name around the world for decades.

Another famous German car company, Bayerische Motoren Werke, more commonly known as BMW, made aircraft engines during World War I, then expanded into motorcycles and sports cars.

But in the 1950s, its future was uncertain until the main shareholders—the Quandt family—took over and made it the automobile power that it is today.

The product of another German car company rivals that of Daimler Benz as the most famous German car in the world. In 1938, Volkswagen (meaning "people's car") started mass production of the automobile designed in 1936 by the Austrian Ferdinand Porsche, and continued to do so after World War II under a dynamic manager, Heinz Nordhoff. The company remained fully nationalized until 1961, but its sales started slipping as people became wealthier and could afford luxury cars. To counter this, it developed the "yuppie car" of the 1980s, the best-selling Volkswagen Golf.

Volkswagen has ties with two other famous cars. First, the company owns Audi, producers of one of the most popular luxury cars in the world. Second, Ferdinand Porsche left Volkswagen and started his own automobile company in the 1950s. Today, sports car lovers admire the sleek design of Porsche, with 50% of its sales to the United States. The company is still run by the Porsche family.

On a sadder note, the former East German company Trabant is a tragic story of car production. It closed down shortly after German reunification when faced with strong competition from the other more established and famous car makers. As a result, 1 million jobs were lost.

The Mercedes Benz factory near Stuttgart.

INDUSTRIES

Germany imports most of its raw materials and energy sources, though it does have profitable bituminous and brown coal (lignite) deposits in the Ruhr and Saar valleys. Its steel industry is concentrated near these areas. It also has small amounts of iron ore, petroleum, and natural gas.

The chemical industry is one of Germany's most important, and includes companies like Bayer, BASF, and Hoechst. Machine and vehicle construction is another major industrial sector which includes aircraft manufacture, shipbuilding, plant machinery and, of course, automobiles.

Electrical engineering, electronics, and office equipment are growing industrial sectors. While many industries are extremely successful, traditional heavy industries such as steel and shipbuilding are, as in other Western countries, suffering a severe decline. Competition from the Japanese and new technology are now reducing the profits enjoyed by German production. The addition of the former East German population to the market economy has put the whole structure in trouble, with industrial output down by 20% in the first year of unification.

AGRICULTURE

As with other Western countries, a decreasing proportion of Germany's population works on the land. Farms are growing larger and are often linked together in cooperatives, though many small-scale operations remain, often run by part-timers with other jobs.

The different regions and soil types are suited to different types of farming. The north coast, with marshy soil rich in nutrients, is suited for dairy farming and some horse breeding. Pasture lands are found on the foothills of the Alps. Poultry, pigs, cattle, and some sheep and ducks are raised in these areas. A fertile belt runs along the southern flank of the lowlands, with crops such as flour and feed grains for livestock, vegetables, sugar beet, fruits, potatoes, and grapes that produce wine. Bavaria, Hesse, Baden-Württemberg, and Rhineland-Palatinate have forestry farming.

Farming in Germany is regulated by the Common Agricultural Policy, which at first encouraged an overproduction of grain crops but is now penalizing this in order to maintain falling farm prices. Fishing in the North Sea is likewise governed by numerous regulations.

Beautiful vineyards above the town of Rüdesheim.

The Deutsche Bank in Frankfurt.

TRADE AND COMMERCE

Wholesale trade continues to flourish in Germany, although many small enterprises have gone out of business because they were unable to offer the services and discounts of larger operators. Retail turnover has been growing, and increasingly self-service operations have replaced more traditional trade outlets.

Foreign trade has been a major factor in Germany's economic success, with a liberal policy aimed at breaking down trade barriers. Machinery, motor vehicles, chemical products, precision and optical goods, and electrical engineering goods are its main exports. Food, drinks, tobacco, and petroleum products are its main imports.

The bulk of Germany's trade is within the European Community. Major trade fairs are held in Hanover, mainly for mechanical and industrial products.

Germany's balance of payments has been positive, with exports exceeding imports in value during the 1980s, though it is experiencing a temporary reverse after reunification.

BANKING AND FINANCE

In the 1970s, Deutsche Bank, Diskont Gesellschaft, and Dresdner Bank—the three major German banks—were founded. Frankfurt remains the banking center of Germany and an international center of finance. The Frankfurt Stock Exchange is one of the world's leading stock exchanges, while other exchanges can be found in Bremen, Düsseldorf, Hamburg, Munich, Hanover, Stuttgart, and Berlin.

EAST AND WEST DISPARITIES

The effects of reunification will take several years to stabilize, and it will be some time before the economic advantages of reabsorbing 17 million people are known. Industries and businesses in the former East have suffered under capitalism, and a number have closed. West German managerial skills have helped some to continue, but the work force there has fewer skills or motivational reasons for succeeding.

At the end of 1990, the gross national product of East Germany was 33% that of West Germany; its industrial productivity 28.5% and its income level 60%. The contrast between factories, industries, and enterprises in the two regions is huge in terms of equipment, working practices, general safety, and productivity levels.

A government organization has been set up to convert 8,000 businesses from state economy to the free market. By October 1991, it had sold nearly 3,000 businesses, a rate of approximately 20 a day. Its effective task is to remodel the entire East German economy.

Cargo ships line the docks of the harbor in Hamburg.

Germany's asylum laws have led 35,000 refugees to enter the country each month to seek protection. This places a heavy strain on the country's economy, which is already suffering from recession and high unemployment. This situation has led to growing support for extreme right-wing groups, which won seats in several state parliaments.

THE PROBLEMS East Germany has huge infrastructure costs to bear, since almost all its housing and buildings are run down and in need of repair. Its agricultural productivity was greatly affected by a communist land reform where all private land holdings over 247 acres were done away with and redistributed into smaller units, run on a cooperative style. How to re-redistribute this land remains a major problem.

The currency unification, whereby former East Germans could exchange their money for West German notes, was completed in June 1991, though not without considerable loss of savings.

Much of the initial rejoicing over reunification has now disappeared as a whole host of problems—mainly social and economic—have emerged. The government found that it was not easy bringing people who had been used to communist systems into capitalism. In the economic race, East Germans lag behind as they try to adapt communist attitudes of job security and constantly being watched to the freedom and individual responsibility of a free market economy.

Some West German employers have been quick to hire the best East German workers, taking away experienced people, particularly in health care and nursing, from the new states.

West German workers, initially pleased to be reunited with their fellow Germans, now feel their jobs threatened by the flood of skilled and semi-skilled workers who are prepared to work for less because they are used to earning less than their Western counterparts. Also, West Germans are paying slightly higher income and indirect taxes for one year in order to fund East German reconstruction.

Xenophobia (fear of foreigners), anti-Semitism, and racism are finding support from some poorer East Germans. There has been an increase in Neo-Nazi attacks on immigrants and rioting has been experienced in a number of cities.

WORKING LIFE

Germany has a powerful set of labor laws protecting workers' rights and giving them a real say in the running of their work places. A system of worker participation in management operates in all steel, mining, coal, and limited and joint stock companies. Companies employing over 2,000 people have an *Aufsichtsrat* ("OWF-sikts-rart"), a council composed of delegates from workers and management. Firms with over five employees must have a *Beitriebsrat* ("Bye-TREEBS-rart"), a workers' council. These councils are consulted over recruitment, dismissals, unemployment, and new technology.

Motor worker Steffi Koch, 22, on the production line.

During the 1930s, the labor movement was divided into over 200 groups, making resistance to Nazism impossible. Today, there are 17 unions within the Deutscher Gewerkschaftsbund—the German union of unions—and they see themselves as guardians of democracy. Roughly 38% of employees are unionized, with about 85 to 90% in the heavy industries.

Unions strive for better conditions, but fear of inflation keeps them from demanding excessive wages. Unions are arranged so that all workers in the same company belong to the same union, to avoid conflicts and duplicating negotiations. Once an annual wage agreement is signed it is like a peace treaty and no strikes take place; during negotiations, there are various procedures, and a strike can take place only with the approval of 75% of the workers voting by secret ballot. Only a union can call a strike.

Germans are traditionally hard working, though reportedly less so than they used to be. They also have the shortest working year in the West after Belgium, with five to six weeks paid vacation and public holidays generally totalling 39 vacation days a year.

GERMANS

ROUGHLY 82 MILLION PEOPLE LIVE IN GERMANY. The birth rate in former West Germany has been falling since 1974, and it is now 1.8 children per couple on average. Germany has the lowest birth rate in the world, and it is a decline that is expected to continue.

The majority of Germans live in the huge conurbations (which are continuous networks of urban communities) of the Rhine-Ruhr valley near Cologne, the Rhine-Main area near Frankfurt, and the Swabian industrial area near Stuttgart.

One in three inhabitants of former West Germany lives in a large town or city; in 1982, 21 million people lived in 68 towns with populations of over 100,000.

Opposite: **A jolly German during the Oktoberfest celebration.**

Left: **Germans relaxing in a square in Munich.**

A crowd gathers to await the 9 a.m. opening of a sale in a popular store in former East Berlin.

GERMAN CHARACTERISTICS

The German nation grew from the different tribes of Franks, Saxons, Bavarians, and Swabians, and these continue to be active regional groups, with some stereotypical characteristics which persist. For example, Rhinelanders are thought to be easy-going, and Swabians thrifty. Those from south Germany, particularly Bavaria, are often conservative, jolly, and generally Roman Catholic; those from the north are generally Protestant, more sophisticated, and liberal. Berliners and Germans from the province of Schleswig-Holstein are reputedly very talkative.

Jokes are never made on serious matters such as politics, nor is it common for Germans to joke about themselves. There is a love for bureaucracy and people obey and rarely question rules. A love of order translates into extreme neatness, and families are often very house-proud.

There is little general feeling of patriotism, and local loyalties are stronger than national ones. Germans are conscious of democracy, taking their responsibilities seriously despite occasional political scandals.

Drinks, anyone? A man seems to be enjoying himself at the Munich Oktoberfest.

A Bavarian in his native costume.

DRESS

In everyday wear, Germans dress the modern Western way: jeans, T- or sweatshirts, leather jackets, and sneakers or leather boots for teenagers and children; Western suits and ties for businessmen; and fashionably tailored suits for female executives. For the fashion conscious there are boutiques with designer clothing in large cities such as Berlin, Hamburg, Munich, and Düsseldorf. While German dress is becoming more casual on the whole, it is still acceptable to dress in full evening dress—long dresses for women, tuxedos or tails for men—when attending formal functions such as the opera or theater performances, as well as high-class clubs and casinos.

Dress variations do exist between the regions. Visible examples are the Baltic Sea blue jacket and trousers with a peaked cap, the Hamburg blue sailor's cap, or the Bavarian dirndl dress and apron. The famous short leather trousers, called lederhosen, are common throughout Germany.

The traditional Munich-style dress is the Bavarian *Tracht* ("TRACT") or loden: green wool capes and jackets. Instead of lederhosen, Bavarian men might wear grey or green trousers with a waterproof woven jacket and a green felt hat topped by a pair of feathers. These costumes are worn during festive occasions, more often in rural than urban areas.

The immigrant Turkish community can be easily identified by its conservatively dressed women who generally wear scarves rather than full head coverings.

IMMIGRANTS AND MINORITIES

Today, there are over 4.6 million foreigners working and living in Germany. The majority of immigrant workers, called *Gastarbeiter* ("GAST-are-byte-er") or "guest workers," are Turks. They are married men who initially came alone, but have since brought their families over and built their own communities within the country where they follow their own religious customs. Berlin has the largest Turkish population outside Turkey.

Other immigrant communities include Yugoslavs, Spaniards, and Italians, with small numbers of Africans and Vietnamese. While these groups have integrated somewhat into German life, the Turks remain wary of mixing with Germans, largely because of their religion.

The reunification of Germany and its unemployment problems, as well as the abundant supply of national unskilled labor, have put pressure on these immigrant communities in the job market, though many have lived in Germany for generations. Many young Turks are unemployed and they have become increasingly frustrated.

Minority students with their classmates in a lecture hall at the University of Rostock.

59

The Alexanderplatz in Berlin, a popular meeting place.

MINORITIES The group that is not represented in large numbers are the Jews. Before 1933, there were 530,000 Jews in Germany; after World War II, barely 25,000 remained. The consequent loss of creative talent, entrepreneurship, and cultural achievement cannot be measured. The guilt the German people feel remains powerful. For instance, Dachau Concentration Camp, where thousands of Jews were murdered by the Nazis, is the fourth most visited site in Germany today.

About 100,000 Sorbians live between the Saale and Oder rivers. Road signs in this region are in both Sorb and German. There is also a small Frisian-speaking minority on the North Sea coast.

Immigrant and minority workers have considerable political rights within Germany today, more than during the 1980s. Unfortunately, there is still racism in Germany, with many families preferring their children to marry fair-skinned people, and gangs of neo-Nazis who beat up Turkish workers. Former East Germans are particularly xenophobic, often because they rarely meet foreigners.

THE WITTELSBACHS

The Wittelsbach family ruled Bavaria from 1180 to 1918, first as dukes and later as monarchs. After World War I, Ludwig III formally gave up the throne and the family gave several castles and works of art to the state of Bavaria.

During the Nazi period in the 1930s and 1940s, the Wittelsbach family, led by Ludwig III's son, Prince Rupert, opposed and resisted Adolf Hitler by producing an opposition newspaper. As a result, many family members were sent to concentration camps.

Today, the family still makes use of the Schloss Nymphenburg castle in Bavaria for particular functions. When Pope John Paul II visited the area in 1980, the duke of Bavaria was among those greeting him.

Some people in Bavaria still call the duke "your royal highness." The Wittelsbach family remains popular in the region; they are closely identified with local traditions and heritage, and remembered as good and kind rulers.

CLASS DIVISIONS

The German aristocracy played a dominant role in society until 1918. They have since been replaced by an industrial class—wealthy industrialists and business people who generally avoid displaying their wealth (except in the fast cars that they drive).

Some traces of the old aristocracy remain if you look hard enough: in the romantic castles and in surnames with the word "von," for example. Such people are generally courteous, cultured, and serious minded, regarding their positions in life as a privilege and attempting to put something back into the community by way of social and charity work.

A shepherd and his sheepdog tending a flock near the Elbe River.

The upper middle class is made up of managers, professionals, and civil servants, while the shrinking lower class has decreased as more and more people attain the education, income, and lifestyle of the middle class. The prevailing nature of German public life is that of the lower middle class.

Social divisions today are based on wealth. The differences are between the employed and the unemployed, and former East and West Germans, with the former earning only 60% of their Western counterparts.

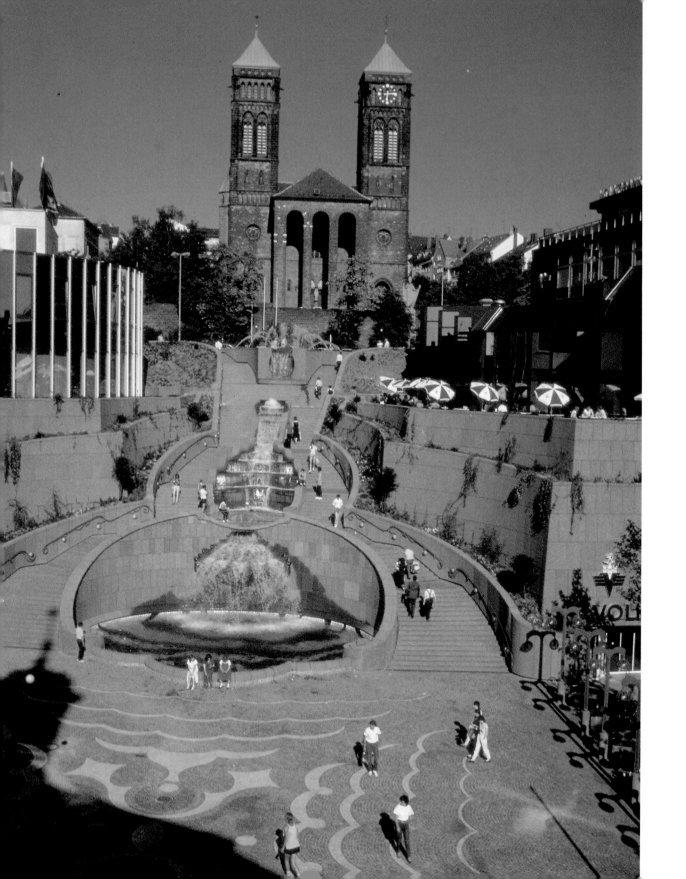

LIFESTYLE

MANY GERMANS SPEND THEIR WORK and leisure time in the same ways as people in other Western countries. Families are generally small and nuclear (which means a social unit composed of only father, mother, and children), particularly in urban areas.

One or even two parents work in order to meet the fairly high cost of living. Young people dress in jeans and watch American television programs and sports.

Within Germany, there remain great varieties of lifestyle—between the urban and the rural, the different localities, the employed and the unemployed, the former East German and the former West German. Some common threads are described in this chapter.

Opposite: **The town of Pirmasens in the Pfälzer Wald.**

Left: **A roadside café in Munich.**

Colorful houses and stores on a street in Dinkelsbühl.

HOUSING

It is part of the German dream to have a house and garden. About 40% of West Germans own their own homes, which generally come with all modern conveniences. Seventy percent of German housing has been built since 1945. Rent and mortgage payments make up a high proportion of a family's monthly expenses.

Architecture styles vary in different areas, depending on local house-building materials and the climate. In the Alpine Foreland, chalet-style houses are built on slopes that face south. In Sauerland, half timbered houses have slates covering their western walls for added protection against the biting wind. Some city residential areas have restored blocks of buildings from the 19th century; other suburban areas have high-rise blocks with poor facilities called *Trabantenstädte* ("Trab-ANT-en-stett-ter").

FAMILY LIFE

In many urban areas both spouses work, mainly because this is the only way they can afford the lifestyle that they desire. The size of the German family is decreasing; on average, a family will have just one or two children. In the rural areas of southern Germany you can still find families with several generations under the same roof. But this is rare in urban areas or farther north, where housing units are too small to include grandparents and relatives outside the immediate family unit.

Young people are relatively free to meet and marry whom they choose, and indeed marriage is not the only option: 40% of couples between the ages of 18 and 35 live together without the civic or religious ceremony of marriage. In urban situations single parents are accepted. Illegitimate children in Germany have the same legal rights as legitimate children.

Family and friends gather in a beer and wine garden in the Rhine valley town of Boppard.

65

Kindergarten children get together for a sing-along session.

CHILDHOOD RITUALS

Christening occurs soon after a baby's birth, whether in a Protestant or Catholic family. Godparents are chosen from those who belong to the same church as the child's parents. The first day at school is an important occasion for all children. For Catholics, the child's first communion at the age of seven is important; for Protestants, confirmation at around 14 is a major occasion.

YOUTH

Although children are treated as mini adults from an early age, Germany is not a particularly child-friendly society in some ways—for example, neighbors often complain if children are noisy. There can be a generation gap; parents who lived through the postwar period often feel their children are too materialistic. Roughly one-third of the population is under 25, and is interested in popular clothing, music, and politics. The problem of drug addiction is found mainly in urban areas.

WEDDINGS

An engagement is seen as an official bond to marry, and both partners wear a gold ring on the fourth finger of the left hand during this time.

There are two parts to a wedding in Germany. First comes the civil ceremony in a registry office, generally the day before the church wedding. That evening the rare custom of *Polterabend* ("POLL-ter-are-bent")— breaking glass and pottery to frighten the devil—is occasionally still practiced.

The second part is the religious ceremony which takes place the next day. Two or three small children bearing flowers, followed by the bride and groom, enter the church together. The gold engagement rings are moved from the left to the right hand of both the bride and groom during the service. After the ceremony there is usually a reception, with food and drinks, speeches, and jokes.

Wedding anniversaries are family celebrations, as are children's birthdays and adults' 60th, 70th, 80th, and 90th birthdays.

DEATHS

Deaths are announced in the newspapers. Relatives send black-rimmed notifications of the funeral arrangements to friends and other acquaintances so they can attend.

Funerals are a time of family reunion and compassion for the deceased's family, though it is rare for a full wake to be held. It is customary for the surviving partner to wear both wedding rings as a sign of widowhood.

Graves are tended to regularly and full mourning dress can be worn for up to six months in some parts of Germany, though this is becoming less common nowadays.

A cross commemorating an East German who was shot while trying to escape to the West.

WOMEN

In the Basic Law women are granted the same legal rights as men, but in employment, they often find these lacking in certain respects. Within marriage, laws protect women's property rights, and by law husband and wife are to come to an agreement over household duties and employment. Husband and wife can choose either the woman's or the man's name, and in the case of divorce, the wealthier partner continues to support the other regardless of who is responsible for the breakup of the marriage.

Women employees are more likely to become unemployed during a recession and fewer are promoted into top posts. While one-third of the Green Party's members are women, other parties have a low number of women members and candidates, often because their local organizations are dominated by men.

Expensive child care costs is one of the reasons why many German women choose not to work. In the former East Germany, child care was provided by the state, enabling over 80% of women to join the work force.

Students in a prestigious art college in Magdeburg learn the finer points of painting and drawing.

The Aachener Strasse, one of the more popular shopping districts in Cologne.

SHOPPING

Large supermarkets and shopping centers are located on the outskirts of towns, accessible by car. Many smaller grocery stores are going out of business because they cannot match the competitive prices of the supermarkets.

Shops close at 6:30 p.m. on weekdays and at 2 p.m. on Saturdays. They are closed on Sundays, following the 1956 Shop Closure Law designed to protect small retailers.

EDUCATION

Education is compulsory for German children from the age of 6 to 16. Religious instruction is taught until the age of 14, when a child is able to choose whether or not to continue.

The school year runs from the end of August to June or July, with a half-year report in February, and two weeks vacation for Christmas and Easter.

A schoolteacher rounding up his students during a school field trip.

The school day is from 8 a.m. to 1 p.m. on Mondays to Fridays, and from 8 a.m. to noon on Saturdays. School hours are spent almost totally on academic subjects, with few non-academic activities. Children return home for lunch after school and do their homework in the afternoons—another reason why there are so few working women, since child care is so costly.

The first school for the German child is the elementary school—*Grundschule* ("GROONT-shoo-ler")—starting at the age of 6, and generally going on for four years, although this varies in each state. Then roughly half of these children progress to secondary school—*Hauptschule* ("HOW-pt-shoo-ler")—and take vocational training.

More academic-minded students go to the intermediate school—*Realschule* ("Ray-ARL-shoo-ler")—for six years before entering a technical school. The most traditional type of grammar school—*Gymnasium* ("Ghimm-NARS-ee-oom")—specializes in the classics, modern languages, or sciences and mathematics. It prepares students to take the *Abitur* (ABB-ee-toor) exam, which is the final step to the university.

Medical students at the Humboldt University in Berlin.

TYPES OF SCHOOL AND FURTHER EDUCATION Roughly 95% of children attend state schools; the rest attend private schools—usually run by churches, or the increasingly popular Waldorf schools for less competitive children. The different states run their own education systems. Although the states appoint teachers in the schools, they are subject to the authority of the Federal Ministry of Education.

Former East German states are gradually changing their educational systems—from a 10-year spell in a standard school to one similar to their western counterparts. It is a gradual process of weeding out communist ideas and philosophy from syllabuses and teaching methods. And in many subjects—modern languages for instance, where Russian rather than English used to be the main foreign language—there is much ground to make up.

Roughly one in four children gets a college education, attending the crowded lecture halls of the various universities in pursuit of a degree. As a result of considerable student unrest during the 1960s, students today have a say in how universities are run.

HEALTH CARE

Health care services in Germany are well funded and equipped, with health insurance for all employees, the self-employed, and their dependents. The lower income groups and the unemployed are helped by state and federal projects. Still, there are occasional health care abuses, such as when insurance or social security funds are used for expenses like visiting spas.

More than half the hospitals in Germany are run by the states and cities; 12% are privately run and 35% are run by non-profit organizations such as churches. Medicine is a popular profession in Germany because it is well paid compared to other countries.

A physician attending to one of her elderly patients.

RELIGION

GERMANY IS A SECULAR STATE, but freedom of religion is guaranteed by the Basic Law and funded by a church tax that people have to contract out of if they don't wish to pay. About 90% of the population do pay this tax.

Although contracting out is a secret matter between the local government *Rathaus* ("RAT-house") and the individual, employers are bound to notice the different amount deducted from employees' pay checks. Contracting out may not look good to a religious employer.

So unlike many other Western countries with a decreasing level of religious practice, Germany's churches are well maintained and funded, and priests, pastors, and vicars live fairly comfortable lives.

Sunday is a day of rest; shops are closed and, in some areas, there are even by-laws forbidding residents from hanging out washing to dry.

Above: **A sculpture of saints and angels on the corner of a building in Bamberg.**

Opposite: **Cologne Cathedral in all its glory at night.**

About 90% of former West Germans are Christians; half are Protestants and the other half Roman Catholics. The former East Germany guaranteed religious freedom. Roughly 80% of its citizens are Protestants, the rest Roman Catholics. However, East Germany had no religious instruction in school, and socialist rites replaced religious ceremonies at birth, marriage, and death.

German Christians pack a church during an evangelical meeting in Berlin.

CHURCH IN SOCIETY

Many leading members of the Protestant and Catholic churches stood up against Adolf Hitler during World War II and, as a result, the churches do see themselves as guarantors of freedom and democracy. This proved to be true again in 1989 when church members played a big part in the downfall of former communist East Germany and the re-emergence of democracy in that part of the country.

Both Protestant and Catholic churches run a variety of social services—schools, kindergartens, nursing homes, handicapped programs, hospitals, and so on—which fill a general social need and are used by people of any or no beliefs.

The country is broadly divided between a mainly Protestant north and a Catholic south. However, the large influx of refugees in 1945, as well as East Germans during the 1940s and 50s, has served to blur these lines and give more communities a truly mixed Christian denomination.

CATHOLICISM

The Catholic areas of West Germany are predominantly in the south: Rhineland-Palatinate, Saarland, and Bavaria, with an equal number of Catholics and Protestants in Baden-Württemberg and North Rhine-Westphalia. In the former West Germany, there are five church provinces with five archbishoprics—Cologne, Paderborn, Munich, Bamberg and Freiburg, and Berlin—and 16 bishoprics. The colorful festivals of Corpus Christi and Ascension Day are celebrated in Catholic areas.

PROTESTANTISM

Protestants in Germany mainly belong to three denominations: Lutheran, Reformed (Calvinist or Zwinglian), and United (a combination of Reformed and Lutheran). Protestantism is practiced predominantly in the north. Churches are grouped into an alliance of 17 state churches known as the Evangelische Kirche in Deutschland (EKD), at the top of which is a synod for legislative matters and a council for executive matters. Most Lutheran churches are also grouped into the United Evangelical Lutheran Church of Germany—or the VELKD.

Inside the cathedral in Cologne.

There are also smaller free churches. The Methodists and the Evangelical community have joined to become the Evangelical Methodist Church. There is an Old Catholic Church and small numbers of Quakers, Mennonites, and the Salvation Army, better known for their social work than for the number of their followers.

MARTIN LUTHER

It was in Germany that Christianity first split into Roman Catholicism and Protestantism. In 1517, Martin Luther, an Augustinian monk, criticized the Catholic Church's money-raising means of selling indulgences to wealthy subscribers in order to fund the building of such beautiful churches as St. Peter's in Rome. Corruption and malpractice were common throughout the church at that time, so Luther argued for equality between layperson and priest, disputed the Pope's authority and the role of the clergy, and asserted the individual's right to read the Scriptures for himself or herself, translating the Bible from Greek to German to help people do so.

Luther's moral protest was adopted for political ends by a number of German princes. His protest against the church's abuse of authority indirectly triggered off the Peasants' Revolt in 1525, which was forcibly put down by the princes. Religious wars in the 16th and 17th centuries killed many Germans and reduced the country to a series of tiny states. The former church unity could not be restored.

OTHER BELIEFS

JUDAISM The Jewish population in Germany before 1933 was about 530,000, but the horrors of the Final Solution and emigration have reduced that number to around 25,000 today. There are 65 Jewish congregations in Germany, the largest in Berlin and Frankfurt (the banking center largely started by Jews). Acts of atonement have been performed by former German leaders at Israel's monuments to the war, and reparations were agreed and paid to Israel during the 1970s. The reluctance of large numbers of Jews to return to Germany has deprived the country of much creative talent. Recently, anti-Semitism has resurfaced in some areas of the country, worrying the majority of the German population.

ISLAM The large Turkish minority mainly centered in Berlin makes up the bulk of Germany's 1.8 million Moslems. Rights of worship, education, and religious schooling are all guaranteed and constantly under review. German employers often set aside rooms to allow Moslem employees to carry out their daily prayers. The Moslem festival of Ramadan and observances and arrangements for the pilgrimage to Mecca are all carried out with the help of religious leaders and government bodies. The German government works with Turkey to bring Islamic religious teachers to Germany to preach to its Turkish minority. They ask for liberal rather than fundamentalist preachers, so that the Turks will have fewer problems integrating into German society.

ATHEISM A significant proportion of German youth are atheist; religion does not come into their daily lives. This is common in urban centers, especially Berlin, and in the former East Germany, where atheism was encouraged and taught, even though religious freedom was allowed.

Despite being a secular state, Christianity still has a great effect on German culture, personal attitudes, the social structure and even politics. The ruling political party, the Christian Democratic Union, is strongly supported by Catholics and Protestants.

LANGUAGE

GERMAN IS SPOKEN THROUGHOUT GERMANY and in parts of neighboring Luxembourg, Switzerland, the Netherlands, and Austria. This common language was a uniting force of the people long before Germany became a nation, and remains a common bond between states and regions today. The language is changing, with increasing additions from Western countries, particularly Britain and the United States.

Together with German, Frisian is spoken along the North Sea coast; Danish just along the frontier with Denmark in Schleswig-Holstein; and Slavonic Sorbian or the Wendish language in parts of Lusatia, Berlin, and east of the Elbe River. Many Germans speak English fluently, and many former East Germans can converse in Russian.

Opposite: **A couple having a conversation in a Munich shopping plaza.**

Left: **"The wall must go,"** says the graffiti on the Berlin Wall.

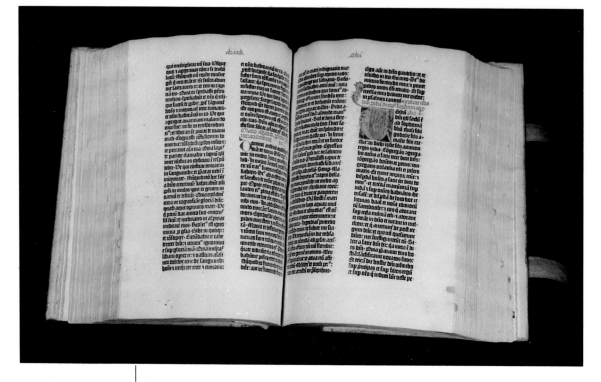

The Gutenberg Bible, which dates from the 1460s, is one of the first printed books in Germany.

THE GERMAN LANGUAGE

Many German words are similar to English words, both in meaning and pronunciation: *gut* (good), *Buch* (book), *fein* (fine), *Haus* (house), *Preis* (price). Perhaps the oddest thing about the language to foreigners is the length of some words. These are generally compound words, which explain a combined and associated meaning but could take a whole phrase in English. Several German words have crept into the English language, for example, wanderlust, rucksack, hinterland, *Weltanschauung*, leitmotif, and abseil.

German grammar can seem overwhelmingly complicated to English speakers. The language uses three different genders (neuter, male, and female) and four different cases (nominative, dative, accusative, and genitive). Each noun starts with a capital letter and any qualifying adjectives agree in gender and case with the noun. German word order is quite unlike English, with the verb of any subordinate clause coming right at the end of the clause rather than immediately after the subject.

SCRIPT

If you look at written German, you may come across a curious sign—"ß"—nowadays written as "ss." This is pronounced "tz." Another is a kind of "f," which is the way an "s" is written at the beginning of a word. Both characters are no longer commonly used in today's newspapers. Several German newspapers use versions of the old German script for their title letterings. Works by Goethe and Schiller originally written in this old style are almost unrecognizable today.

PRONUNCIATION

Pronunciation is generally straightforward, with the stress on the root of a word, often the first syllable. Consonants are broadly pronounced as in English, though some combinations differ. These are listed below.

Letter	Example	Pronunciation
ch	*acht*	guttural "ch" as in Scottish "loch"
chs	*sechs*	"ks" as in "wakes"
d	*and*	"t" as in "wait" at the end of a word, otherwise as in English
pf	*Pferd*	"pf"—no equivalent in English
qu	*Qualität*	"qv"—no equivalent in English
s	*Sie*	"z" as in "zoo" at beginning of a word, otherwise as in English
v	*Vögel*	"f" as in "full" at the beginning of a word, otherwise as in English
w	*Wir*	"v" as in "vex"

One reason why foreigners find it hard to understand German is that a number of words are compounds of smaller words. Different nouns can be joined, such as Rathaus, *which is a compound of* Rat *(parliament) and* Haus *(house). So the compound* Rathaus *means the building where parliament meets.*

83

Vowels and vowel combinations are pronounced differently from English, though they generally follow the rules below.

Letter	Example	Pronunciation
a	*Land*	short "a" as in "hat"
a	*Name*	long "a" as in "father"
ä	*Länder*	"e" sound as in "lender"
ai	*Kaiser*	long "i" as in "height"
au	*Haus*	"ow" as in "house"
äu	*Häuser*	"oy" as in "soil"
e	*Sechs*	short "e" as in "set"
e	*dritte*	unstressed, like "e" in "open"
ee	*Nordzee*	"ay" as in "say"
ei	*weiss*	long "i" s in "white"
eu	*euch*	"oy" as in "soil"
i	*Ich*	short "i" as in "in"
ie	*Sie*	"ee" sound as in "tea"
o	*wo*	long "o" as in "woe"
o	*Doppel*	short "o" as in "on"
ö	*Löffel*	"er" as in "berth"
u	*Buch*	short "u" as in "put"
ü	*Bücher*	fine "u," like "unique" without the "y" sound

As the table shows, vowels with umlauts (two dots over letters) are pronounced differently from those without. When publishers are unable to set umlauts, an extra "e" is added to indicate altered pronunciation (and often meaning). For instance, Bücher can be written as Buecher.

HIGH AND LOW GERMAN

High German is German that is traditionally spoken in southern and central Germany—the regions with the higher terrain—and is now accepted and taught as the standard language. By contrast, Low German is the language spoken on the low, flat northern plain.

The main difference between the two languages was caused by the German Sound Shift, which occurred between the 5th and 8th centuries, whereby the consonants "p," "t," and "k" became "f/pf," "ss/z," and "ch" respectively. Thus:

Low German	*Appel*	*Slapen*	*Water*	*Tid*	*Maken*
High German	*Apfel*	*Schlafen*	*Wasser*	*Zeit*	*Machen*
English	Apple	Sleep	Water	Time	Make

Common German greetings are straightforward, depending on the time of day. Rather than "Hello" or "Hi," Germans say Guten Morgen *("GOO-ten MORR-gen" or good morning),* Guten Tag *("GOO-ten TAARG" or good day) or* Guten Abend *("GOO-ten ARE-bent" or good evening). Goodbye is* Auf Weidersehen *("OWF WEE-der-zay-en" or until we meet again), while between friends and family, a less formal goodbye is* Tschüss *("SCHHU-ss" or see you).*

FORMS OF ADDRESS

In Germany there are different ways of addressing people, depending on how well you know them, their status, age, and so on. The most polite word for "you" (singular and plural) is *Sie*, which you should use until asked to be more familiar—rather like calling someone Mr. or Mrs. Jones in English until you are invited to use their first name. It would not be unusual, or rude, to continue addressing business associates as *Sie*.

First names are rarely used in offices: *Herr* ("HAIR") or *Frau* ("FROW")/ *Fräulein* ("FROW-line") so-and-so remains the form of address at work, and a gulf divides office and private life.

Many German children address their parents as *Sie* to show respect. Close friends, siblings, and parents talking to children use the word *du*, as do many young people, especially in Berlin. Members of the Green Party also seem to have little time for formality.

If someone has a title through a qualification—a lawyer, doctor or professor, for instance—they should be addressed as such to show respect: *Herr Doktor* or *Herr Professor*. Old aristocratic families can be recognized by the "von" in the surname. Some also have titles, as in Baron Manfred von Richthofen, one of Germany's most famous fighter pilots.

BODY LANGUAGE AND ETIQUETTE

Social interaction is often quite formal in Germany. People shake hands when introduced or when greeting people they already know, and are protective of their personal space and privacy.

At mealtimes it is impolite to start eating before your host has wished you *Guten Appetit* ("GOOT-en App-er-TEET"), and you should only drink after hearing the greeting *Prost* ("PROH-st").

THE MEDIA

Germany has 385 daily newspapers, almost all regional, and various constitutional safeguards against any kind of censorship—though, obviously, the papers may reflect the interests of their owners.

Freedom of speech is guaranteed in the Basic Law. This ultimately means that there is some scandal-mongering practiced by the various newspapers in their attempt to woo readers, and these acts often go unpunished.

Among the largest circulation papers are *Die Welt* and the *Frankfurt Allgemeine*, both on the political right; the *Suddeutsche Zeitung*, which has a liberal slant; and the *Bild Zeitung*, the daily tabloid with sensational scoop stories and a circulation of 5.4 million. The major publishing empire, and one of the largest in Europe, is the German Springer group, which publishes many periodicals and newspapers.

ARTS

OVER THE CENTURIES, Germany has been the cradle of much of Europe's music, literature, theater, and fine arts. From Beethoven and Bach to Goethe, Heine, and Schiller, Germany has produced some of the finest musicians and writers in the history of the civilized world. There is a strong local cultural tradition and attendance at musical and theatrical performances is always high.

MUSIC

Germans are passionately fond of music, poetry, and drama. Every small town has a small theater or opera house, its own amateur troupe, an orchestra or small musical group, and maybe a choral society. Music and singing play a big part in social activities and public celebrations.

Above: **The state opera house in Dresden's Theaterplatz.**

Opposite: **Clay figures in the Dresden Art Museum.**

Germany has 72 state or municipally funded orchestras, including famous ones such as the Berlin Philharmonic Orchestra, the Munich Philharmonic, and the Bamberg Symphonic. There are 50 opera houses—of which Hamburg's (founded in 1678) is the oldest—1,000 theaters, and 1,300 museums.

Recordings of classical works under such conductors as Herbert von Karajan for Deutsche Grammophon have sold in the millions worldwide. Radio orchestras reach out to those who are unable to attend live performances. Music and theater festivals occur frequently, celebrating famous local composers, playwrights, or performers.

Music education is strongly supported, with conservatories, music colleges, corps, and councils encouraging young people to develop their talents in performing, as well as in listening to, all types of music. Local choral groups and quartets are active throughout the country.

GREAT MUSICIANS

Music, like language, knows no boundaries, and composers based in Austria such as Wolfgang Mozart, Christoph Gluck, and Franz Haydn are often regarded as part of German musical culture. Some of the major composers who lived and worked in Germany are described here.

Johann Sebastian Bach (1685–1750) was born in Eisenach, Thuringia, and worked as a choir director in Leipzig for much of his life. He came from a musical family, married twice and had 20 children. He composed organ works, toccatas and fugues, orchestral works including the *Brandenburg Concertos*, and church music like the *St. Matthew Passion* in a baroque style.

George Frederick Handel (1685–1759) traveled widely in Italy and England, composing some of the first operas and the famous oratorio, *The Messiah*, as well as the orchestral suites *The Water Music* and *Music for the Royal Fireworks*.

Ludwig van Beethoven (1770–1827) was born in Bonn and studied under Haydn and Mozart in Vienna. He brought the subjective expression and emotion of the Romantic movement to traditional musical forms. His prolific work included 32 piano sonatas, five piano concertos, nine symphonies, 17 string quartets, one opera (*Fidelio*), and numerous overtures. He became deaf at the age of 30 and was thus unable to hear many of his works performed.

After Beethoven, the Romantic movement continued to flourish. Felix Mendelssohn (1809–1847) traveled widely in Britain and Italy, composing the overture *Fingal's Cave* and the *Fourth "Italian" Symphony* as a result.

Robert Alexander Schumann (1810–1856) composed numerous piano works and much chamber music, as well as four symphonies. Richard Wagner (1813–1886) intensified the emotional content of Beethoven in his numerous operatic works. Johannes Brahms (1833–1897) developed a classic Romantic style in his four symphonies, two piano concertos, and other works.

Richard Strauss (1864–1949), a successor to Wagner, wrote operas that include *Der Rosenkavalier* and many instrumental pieces. Paul Hindemith (1895–1963) composed different types of post-Romantic instrumental music. Carl Orff (1895–1982) wrote operas and dramatic works, including *Carmina Burana*, based on a 13th-century collection of songs from Bavaria. Two influential German composers who are still working today are Hans Werner Henze (b. 1926) and Karlheinz Stockhausen (b. 1928), both leaders in their fields.

BEETHOVEN'S SYMPHONIES

Ludwig van Beethoven's nine symphonies were a radical departure from previous musical styles. They were loaded with emotion and developed themes at length.

The *Third Symphony* was originally dedicated to Napoleon Bonaparte, but was altered when the Frenchman's violent and cruel nature became apparent to Beethoven. So the composer named it instead the *Sinfonia Eroica*, or heroic symphony, in memory of a great man.

The *Fifth Symphony*, written against a military background between 1804 and 1808, is called the *Victory Symphony*. It has one of the most famous openings in all of music: the Morse code for victory—three short notes followed by a long one.

The *Sixth Symphony* or *"Pastoral" Symphony* has a rural theme, and opens with a spring-like awakening in which bird songs can be heard. *The Ninth "Choral" Symphony* contains the rousing setting of Schiller's *Ode to Joy* in its final choral movement.

THE BAYREUTH FESTIVAL

In 1872, the small Bavarian town of Bayreuth offered composer Richard Wagner a permanent theater for his works to be performed. Four years later, *The Ring Cycle* of operas (comprising *Rhinegold*, *The Valkyrie*, *Siegfried,* and *The Twilight of the Gods*) was performed there; and in 1882, the *Parsifal* opera was first staged there.

Every summer a Richard Wagner Festival is held in Bayreuth, organized by his grandson Wolfgang, where modern productions of his works are performed.

JAZZ

In the 20th century, a German jazz school emerged and with it an annual jazz festival in Berlin providing a focal point for artists. The emergence of "free jazz" in the 1960s led to musical improvisation, with such musicians as Alexander von Schlippenbach, Albert Mangelsdorff, Manfred Schoof, Peter Brotzmann, Gunter Hampel, and Heiner Goebbels at the forefront.

POP AND ROCK

Pop and rock bands such as Interzone, Einsturzende Neubauten, Die Arzte, Trio, and Cosa Rosa have had international success. Other successful musicians include Udo Lindenberg, who sings predominantly German rock music, and the pop group Tangerine Dream, which relies heavily on electronics. Meanwhile Germany's Gregorian chants of the 8th and 9th centuries have made a surprising comeback in the pop charts, adapted by the group Enigma.

MOVIES

In the 1920s, Fritz Lang was one of the leading names in German cinema, along with Ernst Lubitsch, F.W. Murnau, and G.W. Pabst.

During the Hitler years, there was a break in creativity and, as a result, immediately after the war the movie industry was not important enough for urgent reconstruction. But in the 1960s, the Young German Film movement, echoing in some ways France's New Wave, took place. Creative individuals such as Alexander Kluge, Volker Schlöndorff, Rainer Werner Fassbinder, and then Werner Herzog and Wim Wenders all came into the forefront of the industry.

Some of the best German movies include Kluge's *Yesterday's Girl*, which depicts how an East German failed to adapt to life in the West; Fassbinder's *Berlin Alexanderplatz* and *The Marriage of Maria Braun*, which show personal suffering and the emotional cost of rebuilding a nation; Schlöndorff's *The Tin Drum*, which was praised all over the world and won the Best Foreign Film Award in 1980. (Incidentally, Schlöndorff's wife, Margarethe von Trotta, is currently Germany's leading woman filmmaker.)

Herzog, hailed as one of the best contemporary directors in the world, often fills his movies with mysticism and a bizarre and subtly exotic quality. One of his best known movies, the monumental *Aguirre, the Wrath of God*, shows a crew of actors in the Peruvian jungle in a bizarre attempt to pull a ship across America.

Film production is generously funded through agreements with television companies and by a series of film awards, although German television is not government-owned but controlled by the states. Still, German "TV movies" have enjoyed their most creative output in recent years, culminating in the epic *Heimat* by Edgar Reith, a depiction of life through three generations of Germans in the North German plain.

THEATER

In the 17th and 18th centuries, the individual German kingdoms set up their own state theaters and encouraged and competed for the best playwrights and actors. Today there are over 350 theaters in Germany, mostly state owned. They receive a lot of aid so that performances are affordable for the average member of the public.

German drama really started with Gotthold Ephraim Lessing (1729–1781), Johann Wolfgang von Goethe (1749–1823), and Friedrich Schiller (1759–1805). Goethe was a voice of the Romantic movement, emphasizing the emotional, unpolitical individual, with terror lurking just beneath the surface of a peaceful scene. Schiller felt that the 18th-century theater had a moral role to instruct the audience, a viewpoint felt by Germans today. Their works are frequently performed in German theaters, along with works by William Shakespeare.

Later German dramatists include Bertolt Brecht (1898–1956) and Peter Weiss (1916–1982), whose play, *Marat/Sade*, was a revolutionary theatrical statement. Günter Grass's highly political play, *The Plebeians Rehearse the Uprising*, is based on the 1953 uprising in East Germany and follows Schiller's idea of the playwright's role to instruct. Heiner Muller's plays continue to analyze Germany's past and present, while Harald Mueller's *Totenfloss* concerns a vision of the world after a nuclear disaster.

Open air theaters spring up throughout Germany during the summer to attract tourists and locals. The Mulheim Theater Days Festival stages new plays each year.

The Goethe monument, in honor of Johann von Goethe, the great German poet and playwright.

THE PLAYS OF BERTOLT BRECHT

Brecht was a prolific playwright who developed his own style of "epic theater." His plays imitated the deeds of humanity through an "alienation device," presenting familiar events and actions in a strange way, but generally avoiding either to applaud or condemn these actions. It was left to the audiences to judge the right or wrong of the situations presented, a judgment that Brecht hoped audiences would continue to act on when they left the theater.

He founded a school literary magazine at the age of 15, writing short pieces and his first play in his late teens. His early ideas and beliefs were destroyed by World War I, and his experience of war shows in *Baal* and *Drums in the Night*. Brecht wrote numerous plays during the 1920s, including *In The Jungle* and *The Rise and Fall of the City of Mahagonny*, as well as a series of short pieces for small groups of performers without an audience. The most famous play from this period was *The Threepenny Opera*, a satirical depiction of life among beggars.

Two plays written in 1931 when he had become a Marxist, *The Mother* and *Saint Joan of the Stockyards*, were hardly performed at that time since they were highly critical of the failing Weimar Republic. *Saint Joan* was used as a chilling example to show how capitalism could exploit people.

Brecht left Germany in February 1933—the day after a fire destroyed the German parliament and showed the true nature of the Nazi regime—traveling to Denmark, Sweden, Finland, the Soviet Union, and finally to the United States. In exile, he developed the theory that the beginning of fascism was in the economic crisis of capitalism. He produced anti-fascist plays like *Round Heads and Pointed Heads* (which saw racism as a diversion from the real contest between exploiters and exploited) and *The Resistible Rise of Arturo Ui* (a comical parody of Hitler's rise, showing the links between big business and fascism).

Some very famous plays were written in this period: *The Life of Galileo* and *Mother Courage and Her Children*, both warning of Nazism; *The Good Woman of Szechuan* with its Marxist message that the good in every person is destroyed by alienation; and *The Caucasian Chalk Circle*, a complicated play within a play where good ultimately triumphs.

Brecht returned to Berlin in 1948, where he set up a theater ensemble and continued to write, while becoming increasingly unhappy about the culturally repressive East German regime. He died of a heart attack in 1956.

LITERATURE

In German literature, the *Niebelungslied* ("NEE-ber-loongs-leet") poem, written around 1200, is considered an early milestone, telling of the dispersal of the German people.

Three centuries later, Martin Luther, the founder of Protestantism, translated the Bible into German at the same time that the printing press was developed, thereby greatly widening the use of written German.

An illustrated Cranach Bible, which has a good example of the old German script.

During the 19th century several German writers emerged. One was Theodor Fontane, a popular social novelist; another was poet Rainer Maria Rilke, who wrote around the turn of the century. After the German Empire was founded in 1871, there was a massive wave of writers who wrote about German patriotism and nationalism, until philosopher Friedrich Nietzsche's ideas criticized these values.

After World War I, the Weimar Republic boasted several Expressionist writers such as Thomas Mann, whose *Buddenbrooks* and *Death in Venice* were highly successful; Herman Hesse, who won a Nobel Prize in 1946; and Franz Kafka, whose works like *The Trial* and *The Castle* portrayed humanity's powerlessness in life—an eerie warning of Nazism.

Modern German writers, many of whom explored the guilt and angst of being German, include Günter Grass, who sees the role of a writer as a highly political one. In the 1990s he remains a lone voice speaking critically of German reunification.

Another is Heinrich Boll, whose *Billiards at Half Past Nine* was published the same year as Grass' *Tin Drum*. A third honored writer is Christa Wolf, whose *The Quest for Christa T* showed just what people could expect from life in former East Germany.

St. Christopher, an engraving by Albrecht Dürer.

FINE ARTS

There are 1,500 museums and art galleries throughout Germany. Many hold frequent exhibitions, which are 86% publicly funded, with organizations such as BMW taking an interest in sponsorship possibilities.

Famous German artists include Albrecht Dürer, in many ways a Renaissance man who was a talented goldsmith, writer, painter, and graphic artist. He is known today mainly for his woodcuts and engravings. Others, such as Hans Holbein the Elder and Hans Holbein the Younger, were successful portrait painters; while Lucas Cranach, a friend of Martin Luther, became an official Reformation painter. Another was Caspar David Friedrich, who was an outstanding Romantic artist.

In the early 20th century the Expressionist movement flourished until it was banned under Nazism. Some of the champions of this movement include Ernst Barlach, who showed human suffering in sculptures; painter Wassily Kandinsky, who lived in Munich and developed an abstract color art; and the Swiss artist Paul Klee, who brought the Cubist movement to Germany, concentrating on form rather than subject. A whole abstract school developed in Munich. A leading abstract artist was Max Ernst, who used collage techniques and Dadaism to start the German Surrealism movement after World War I. His paintings from 1936 to 1938 gave his audience a hint at the horrors of Nazism.

More recent artists include Joseph Beuys, who uses action art with social and political dimensions; Georg Baselitz, known for his upside-down work; Markus Lupertz, for his 1970s painting motifs inspired by German ideology; Gerhard Richter, whose pictures are based on photographs and abstracts; and Bernd Kobeling, whose art themes are from nature.

ARCHITECTURE

Germany's architecture is beautifully varied, from the Gothic styles of Cologne cathedral to the expansive baroque designs of Potsdam's Sans Souci Palace and the Neoclassicist shapes of Berlin's Schauspielhaus. Sadly, much of the former East German architecture has been destroyed, not just by bombs during World War II, but by years of neglect which have led to many buildings being torn down. Hopefully, reunification will save the remaining treasures from a similar fate.

The Bauhaus style of Walter Gropius was a successful and influential style of the 1920s. It concentrated on function, uniting engineering and art.

There are some outstanding modern buildings in Germany today, including the magnificent BMW building designed by Karl Schwanzer; the Stuttgart television tower by Frits Leonhardt; the new Philharmonie in Berlin by Hans Scharoun; and the Gallery of the Twentieth Century by Ludwig Mies van der Rohe.

LEISURE

THE HIGH STANDARD of living in Germany allows its people a lot of leisure time and activity. With up to five weeks of vacation a year, families often spend the summer at the beach—whether it be on the Baltic or North Sea coasts, or abroad on the Mediterranean.

Germans spend leisure time during the work week in a variety of ways, and generally belong to several hobby clubs that reflect their interests. Leisure activities in Germany account for about 20% of the average person's spending, and leisure has itself become an important industry. There is even a German Leisure Association which researches leisure spending, patterns of behavior, and gives out information. It is now even possible to study leisure teaching in some German universities.

Opposite: **German tourists visiting the Solingen Schlossburg Castle.**

Left: **Two children riding their bicycles along the bicycle path by the Rhine River in Düsseldorf.**

Sailing is a popular sport in Hamburg.

SPORTS

One in three Germans is a member of a sports club and spends a lot of time preparing for his or her particular sport. Schools benefit from a government funding program that improves sports facilities, gyms, athletic tracks, and swimming pools.

Gymnastics has been popular since the 19th century and is now funded by the German Sports Aid Foundation, an organization that is funded by private donations and lottery and is not run by the government. Whereas the former East Germany used to invest large sums in training athletes, funding is now scarcer in the new Germany.

Jogging is popular as a cheap and quick sport for those trying to keep fit. For those who prefer swimming, large public pools are found in all big cities, including several spa pools and the Olympic Pool in Munich.

Handball, volleyball, squash, basketball, and cycling all remain popular. There is also an interest in Grand Prix racing; a race in the Eifel Mountains near Heidelberg takes place every year.

SOCCER

Soccer is the most popular participatory and spectator sport in Germany. With its superb sports facilities, it is no wonder the country can produce such good players and teams. The former West Germany won the World Cup three times—in 1954, 1974, and most recently in 1990. It was also runner-up three times, in 1966, 1982, and 1986.

In 1954, they overcame all odds to beat a Hungarian team that is still considered by many to be the greatest team ever assembled in soccer history.

In 1974, the West German team received a rude shock when they were beaten by East Germany in an opening round match. It was the only time the two Germanys played each other in a competitive game. But with legendary stars like Franz Beckenbauer, Gerd Muller, Sepp Maier, and Paul Breitner, the team bounced back, playing tenacious and opportunistic soccer to win the championship by beating Holland, the favorite.

The 1990 team, which beat Argentina, was coached by Beckenbauer, captain of the 1974 team. West Germany also won the European Championship in 1976 and 1982.

Top league clubs like Bayern Munich, Kaiserslautern, and Cologne compete regularly in European competitions, with Bayern being the most successful. Many current top players have even gone overseas to play in the Italian League, to pit their skills against other leading players.

In the domestic league, most games are played on Saturday afternoons, and television excerpts are shown on Saturday evenings.

Former East German teams have recently joined the league as part of reunification. In addition, several former East German stars have been asked to play for the national team as well as for existing teams in a shakedown of the former structure.

Soccer is a popular school sport, with different regional school leagues and a national championship which draws a large crowd. At the professional level, there is a national league, or Bundesliga, which has 16 teams that compete annually. There is also a lower division which has 20 teams. At the end of each season, the top two teams in the lower league swap places with the bottom two of the Bundesliga.

TENNIS

Boris Becker and Steffi Graf have put German tennis on an international footing, equalling such powerhouses as the United States and Sweden.

Becker turned professional at the age of 15 and won the Wimbledon singles title in 1985 when he was just 17. He won the prestigious competition again the following year. He has also won the US Open and the Australian Open. Graf made a name for herself in the late 1980s, reaching her peak in 1988 when she won the tennis Grand Slam—all of the four top competitions in the world.

In 1989, West Germany beat Sweden in the Davis Cup to become the champion tennis nation. The next year, a West German double effort saw Graf and Becker take the Wimbledon singles titles yet again.

An upcoming star to rival Graf and Becker is Michael Stich. He was the country's youth champion in 1984, and turned professional in 1988 at the age of 20, having completed his schooling and taken his *Abitur* exam. He became the second German Wimbledon singles champion in the last decade when he won the competition in 1991. Another up and coming star is Karl Ube Steeb.

German international success in the sport has spurred tennis playing throughout the country and numerous new tennis clubs have sprung up.

THE GREAT OUTDOORS

Germans love to take up a wide variety of activities that will bring them closer to the freedom of the hills and forests. Hiking, walking, and rock climbing are all popular pastimes during weekends and holidays, particularly in the hills of southern Germany.

The alpine lifestyle of fresh air and healthy food is a real part of German folklore. There are well-marked hiking trails in the Alps with mountain huts providing food and shelter along the way for people on long hikes. Boy scout trips and outdoor camps in the hills have traditionally been part of the school system. And adventurous mountaineers can attempt to scale the Zugspitze or one of the smaller peaks.

Horse riding is also popular, especially in the Rhineland-Palatinate, Neckar valley, and Franconia. Activities involving water are also popular: boating trips are available on the Moselle and Neckar rivers; sailing and windsurfing are practiced on the North and Baltic seas and on the Mecklenburg lakes; and canoeing takes place on the Neckar and Lahn rivers and in the Black Forest. In the Bavarian rivers, trout fishing is common while salmon is found in the Danube. Deep-sea fishing trips can be organized from Heligoland in the North Sea.

Vacationers can take the ski lift to the top of the Zugspitze, where they can have a spectacular view of the German Alps.

Opposite: **Vacationers taking chair lifts up a mountain in the German Alps.**

The most popular German card game is skat, which was developed in the early 19th century. Three players use a pack of 32 cards and start bidding. The winning bidder takes on the other two players and has to win more than half the available points in order to win the game.

WINTER SPORTS

Skiing is popular and possible during most winters where there is snow. The Alps is the main skiing area, and while most of the accessible slopes and facilities are in neighboring Austria, the sport remains extremely popular. The town of Garmisch-Partenkirchen is the skiing center of Germany and extremely popular as a weekend excursion from Munich and other southern cities. Cross-country skiing is popular in the Bavarian and Thuringian forests, along with tobogganing, bobsleding, and curling. Skating is another popular pastime, especially on the frozen Bavarian lakes and Hamburg's network of waterways.

The country's superb training facilities have helped Germany be internationally competitive in winter sports. It is precisely these factors that have enabled the country to produce such outstanding winter sports superstars as Katarina Witt, who with her breathtaking ice skating won numerous championships, including Olympic gold medals in 1984 and 1988. And in the 1992 Winter Olympics at Albertville in France, Germany dominated the games, winning the most medals.

AT HOME

Reading books, magazines, and the country's many local newspapers are common forms of relaxation, along with watching television. Card games are popular, especially bridge and skat.

DIY (do-it-yourself) home improvement is an increasingly popular leisure activity. Growing vegetables and flowers in plots, often on the outskirts of towns though sometimes near town centers, is another form of relaxation for many apartment occupants without gardens. And, of course, the car-loving Germans love to clean, polish, and maintain their vehicles, then drive them to visit friends or explore the countryside.

VACATIONS

The generous amount of annual leave from work, as well as school breaks, allows most Germans to take a family vacation for at least two weeks a year. Germans enjoy traveling and exploring different countries—whether it be the beaches of the Mediterranean from Spain to Greece, or as far away as Asia, Africa, and North America.

Vacationing by the seaside is most popular among Germans, especially for those interested in water sports. Many also enjoy meeting people and sampling the local cuisine of countries that they visit.

Germans are the world's greatest tourists, traveling mainly to Austria, Italy, and Yugoslavia, as well as Greece, France, and resorts around the Mediterranean Sea. In 1980, two-thirds of West Germans had their vacations overseas. There are even package tours catering especially to German tourists, with German food and beer on sale at resorts such as Rimini in Italy, and Benidorm in Spain.

Travel restrictions imposed on former East Germans proved annoying for a people who love to travel and see exotic places, and triggered the first steps of the peaceful revolution of 1989. Within Germany, vacations can be spent in the Black Forest, the Alpine foothills, at inland lakes such as the Bodensee or the Chiemsee, and on Sylt Island near Denmark.

A hotel and winehouse in Assmannshausen, a town in the Rhine valley which produces good red wine. The town also has special waters which some people believe can cure rheumatism.

A casino on the Reeperbahn in Hamburg at night.

CLUBS

Germans from all walks of life form clubs—called *Vereine* ("Fer-INE-er")—for their hobbies, political interests and social activities, and pay regular memberships for the privilege.

Bridge clubs, fishing clubs, sports clubs, and local residents' committees—all are favored means of passing the time. These clubs have highly organized and bureaucratic procedures for electing leaders, treasurers, and the like, another example of democratic principles working at the local level. One emigrating farmer belonged to as many as 33 such organizations, all of which he had to resign from before leaving Germany.

Many Germans also form pressure groups. These groups campaign on a number of matters, including road planning, conservation, environmental pollution, and the dangers of nuclear power. Such groups are very successful and participation is high, particularly when they are addressing a matter of local concern.

NIGHT ENTERTAINMENT

Beer cellars can be found in the major cities, especially in Frankfurt and Berlin. Drinking with colleagues and friends is a common social habit, particularly among men who would probably eat at home with the family before downing several glasses of beer or wine with friends. A number of city centers also have cabaret and revue acts, as well as theater and cinema performances. Some are huge places with long trestle tables while others are smaller but more intimate.

Fishing, sailing, and boating are popular leisure activities on the Aussenalster in Hamburg.

FESTIVALS

GERMANY DOES NOT BOAST ANY NATIONAL FESTIVAL, not even a national day, though it does celebrate the reunification of the country on October 3. However, the country has a rich variety of festivities in each state or city which do much to dispel any notion of the Germans being humorless. Many such festivals date from ancient times and have been revived as part of local heritage and tourism in the 20th century.

Folk festivals, often with a Christian focus, take place in towns and villages once a year, with traditional entertainment, handicraft stalls, and dancing. Many pre-Christian rituals survive in these festivals. For instance, the summer solstice of June 24 is linked to the Feast of St John the Baptist, but the practice of rolling burning wheels down hills is not Christian.

Opposite: **Decorating the may tree is a Bavarian spring custom.**

Left: **A popular "Viking" swing ship at a Hamburg fair.**

Masks of all shapes and sizes appear during the carnival in Freiburg.

CARNIVAL

Tied into pre-Christian fertility rites and pagan beliefs, the pre-Lenten carnivals take place mainly in Catholic parts of Germany. People celebrate by wearing terrifying masks that resemble witches, spirits, and demons, as well as taking part in costume balls and dress competitions.

One of the more famous carnivals takes place in Cologne, where 105 different local associations elect three people to dress up as the Carnival Prince, the Peasant, and the Virgin for the duration of the carnival. These characters, usually middle-aged businessmen, wear costumes and throw toffees at the crowd from their privileged positions in the major parades.

Cologne's carnival starts at precisely 11:11 a.m. on November 11, but gets into full swing during the Tolle Tage ("TOLL-er TARG-er") or Crazy Days, just before Lent. The Thursday before Lent is known as Women's Day. This is the day when women can cut off the ties of any men within reach.

On Sunday a big informal procession takes place, with the main procession on Monday, called Rosenmontag ("ROWS-en MONN-targ"). This includes a jester's speech with funny references to local and national politics. Local songs are chanted by the large crowd as the processions go by.

Munich's carnival has a young couple dressed as the *Prinz* and *Prinzessin* (prince and princess), who take part in a stylish procession which includes a dance on Shrove Tuesday by the women of the fruit and vegetable market.

In the town of Elzach in southern Germany's Black Forest masked "fools" run through the town wearing large decorated hats and hitting people with blown up hogs' bladders. In Rottweil rival groups of "fools" jump through the town's Black Gate at 8 a.m. Meanwhile, jesters' banquets are held in Stockach and Grosselfingen, as well as in Lindau on Lake Constance.

THE MUNICH OKTOBERFEST

Every year since October 12, 1810, there has been a beer festival in the brewing capital of Munich. It started as a horse race celebrating the marriage of Bavarian Crown Prince Ludwig I and Princess Therese von Sachsen-Hildburghausen of Saxony. The event was attended by 40,000 people.

In the following years, the race was combined with the state agricultural fair, and booths serving food and drinks were introduced. By the 20th century these booths had developed into large beer halls.

Today, the festival lasts 16 days, ending on the first Sunday of October. The central attraction is 13 huge beer

During the Oktoberfest, the beer tents in Munich are filled with hundreds of people all the time.

tents where you can drink beer from huge quarter-gallon glasses. After a couple of these, people will jump on the benches and tables and sing traditional drinking songs while waitresses bustle between the long tables bringing additional drinks. Outside the beer tents, there are side shows, a fun fair, trinket stalls, and musical performances as well as a range of food stalls. During the 1985 Oktoberfest, 1.3 million gallons of beer, 630,000 barbecued chickens, 65,000 pigs, and 72 oxen were consumed.

OTHER DRINKING FESTIVALS

Other regions have their own beer or wine festivals to celebrate successful harvests. In Stuttgart during the Volksfest, a type of harvest festival, up to 1.5 million gallons of beer and 300,000 chickens are consumed. The festival has been held each year since 1840. In Erlangen, the Bergkirchweih ("BURG-keersh-why") festival starts on the Thursday before Whitsun and lasts 12 days, with beer sampling, brass bands, and fairground entertainment.

In Rhineland there are various local wine festivals. During November wine makers put brooms outside their doors as a signal that their wine is ready. They will then turn their homes into drinking places for a couple of months.

The streets are filled with people whenever there is a fair or festival. This festival is in Hamburg.

VARIOUS FESTIVALS

In northern Germany there are regular horse festivals, including contests like medieval jousting, which generally take place around Whitsun. Roland's Riding, a wooden figure turned on an axis where competitors try to stay on, is a festival that takes place at Kiel and Dithmarschen.

Mounted processions are held during religious celebrations. For instance, the Kötztinger Pfingstritt ("CURTS-tinger PFING-stritt") on Whit Monday involves 500 costumed horses and riders riding four miles to an open-air Mass. One festival remembers the blood Jesus Christ shed and is celebrated with mounted processions in Bad Wurzach and Weingarten, while other celebrations that involve horse riding take place on days that honor particular saints.

Shooting festivals take place from May to August, the largest of which is in the city of Hanover in July. This folk festival lasts 10 days during which over 5,000 marksmen march and compete. Another festival, called Shepherds' Run, is held annually near Stuttgart in August. There, huge processions and open-air dancing combine with an event where competitors run 150 to 300 yards barefoot over stubble. The winner is chosen king of the shepherds.

The Tanzelfest in the Allgäu is one of many medieval celebrations in Germany. It lasts for 10 days and has historical dances and costumes. In the town of Hamelin there is a re-enactment of the Pied Piper legend annually. Some people celebrate Walpurgis Night on April 30; they believe that witches and the devil congregate in the Harz Mountains that night. In autumn, the Rhineland in Flames is a festival with endless firework displays.

The different clubs and societies have their annual festivities and championships. Labor Day is celebrated on May 1, and the next-to-last Sunday in November is Remembrance Day.

In Bleigiessen on New Year's Eve, Germans celebrate a strange festival that dates from pre-Christian times: they pour hot lead into cold water to look at the future!

115

CHRISTIAN FESTIVALS

Epiphany on January 6 is a holiday in predominantly Roman Catholic southern Germany. In the countryside, children dress up as the three kings, wearing the letters C (for Caspar), M (Melchior), and B (Balthasar).

Good Friday is a public holiday and many Christians fast or don't eat meat on that day. On Easter Sunday children search for the Easter Hare and eat decorated hard-boiled eggs. Easter Monday is the time for egg-rolling competitions, and many Catholics take their first communion on the first Sunday after Easter.

Ascension Day is a public holiday, with Catholic processions and the blessing of crops. Corpus Christi is celebrated only in Catholic areas, with elaborate altars and flower pictures along roads, together with processions of statues and relics.

The last day of October is the Protestant celebration of Reformation Day. November 1 (All Saints Day) and November 2 (All Souls Day) are times for tidying church graveyards and laying new wreaths. November 10 is St. Martin's Day when Protestant churches hold celebrations honoring Martin Luther, and Catholics honor a saint with the same name.

Christmas celebrations are family affairs. On December 5 children leave shoes outside their rooms to be filled by "Saint Nicholas." Families put an advent wreath on the table and decorate their homes with fir branches, while children open advent calendars each morning as Christmas approaches.

A bric-à-brac trinket market is found in many town squares before Christmas to provide an opportunity to buy last-minute goodies for family celebrations. The main celebration is on Christmas Eve, rather than Christmas Day. The Christmas tree is decorated on Christmas Eve and gifts are exchanged after a church service.

OBERAMMERGAU PASSION PLAYS

In 1632 there was a plague that wiped out many villages in the Bavarian Alps. As the plague approached the village of Oberammergau ("Oh-ber-AMM-er-gow"), the villagers prayed and promised to perform a passion play every 10 years if they were spared. Miraculously, the plague stopped short of the village. Since then, every 10 years—the next performance will be in the year 2000—countless numbers of Christians, theatergoers, and tourists flock to this tiny mountain hamlet to watch a day-long re-enactment of Christ's death on the cross, performed by virtually the whole village.

FOOD

GERMANY HAS A RICH VARIETY OF FOOD AND DRINK, much of which is grown or produced at home. Combinations of richly spiced meats and salted fish, accompanied by vegetables and washed down with wine or beer, are German delights.

Although the country's cuisine revolves around red meat, there is now an increasing number of vegetarian restaurants throughout the country. Germans also eat little snacks between meals when they are hungry and occasionally have large banquets.

In different regions the same food may come in different styles. You cannot order exactly the same dish in Bavaria as you would in Schleswig-Holstein, but both are worth trying.

Opposite: **A food vendor playing a hurdy-gurdy to attract customers.**

Left: **Goods displayed in a Munich wine and cheese store.**

A wide variety of fresh fruits and vegetables is sold at a Munich market.

LOCAL SPECIALITIES

In German cuisine there are over 200 types of wurst, the sausage made from veal, pork, brain, mustard, spices, and curries. Each region has its own type, from the Bavarian white sausage with parsley and onion to the grilled chipolata.

Blood pudding, poultry cutlets coated with breadcrumbs, cuts of beef and venison, smoked and pickled herring from the North Sea, pickled cabbage or sauerkraut, a potato salad called *Kartoffelsalat* ("Car-TOFF-el-sall-ART"), spiced red cabbage, and mushrooms are found throughout the country, prepared in different ways.

A rich selection of breads is served in restaurants and bought daily in bakeries. Many love the rich, dark rye Pumpernickel breads, with a slightly bitter aftertaste.

Certain areas, especially Baden-Württemberg, Moselle, Franconia, and Bavaria, are particularly concerned about good food. These are wine producing areas. Some local specialities include eel, plum and vegetable soup, and fresh herrings in Hamburg; *Hoppel Poppel*, a potato and ham omelette, in Berlin; suckling pig and roast knuckle of pork in Bavaria; ham eaten with Pumpernickel bread in Westphalia; boiled or breaded fried fish, particularly catfish from the Danube, near Passau; numerous varieties of sausage in Nuremberg; and green herb sauce with pork chops or beef in Frankfurt.

Other favorite foods include Bavarian flour dumplings called *Klossel* ("CLOSS-el"), and Swabian noodles resembling Italian flat noodles served as a side dish with meat or vegetables. Radish from Bavaria is also a popular snack, particularly as an accompaniment to beer.

MEALS

Breakfast is eaten around 7 a.m., or even earlier, in order for children to be at school and adults at work by 8 a.m. A full breakfast includes a variety of breads, sausages, salami and cold meats, along with cheeses and perhaps some jam for a sweet taste, washed down with coffee, tea or fruit juice. More typically, most families simply have fresh rolls, jam, and butter to start a normal day.

Lunch, which is the main meal of the day, is from 11:30 a.m. to 2 p.m. or whenever school is over, and consists of a cooked meal with vegetables. A working parent will usually have a hot meal at the office canteen or a nearby restaurant.

The evening meal is generally quite light. In the south, it consists of a hot meal of sausage, some potato salad, and soup; in the north, it is cheese, cold meats, and salad. The working classes generally eat around 5:30 to 6 p.m.; the middle classes at around 7 p.m. An early evening meal allows people time for their various leisure pursuits, like reading or watching television.

THE RHEINHEITSGEBOT

The German beer industry has been heavily regulated since the 16th century, in order for beer to be of a high quality. A Bavarian government decree of 1516—the *Rheinheitsgebot* ("RHINE-hites-ger-boht")—declared that beer should only contain malt, hops, water—and nothing else. This standard has been adopted throughout Germany over the centuries as a guarantee of high quality. Since Germany is a member of the European Community, beers from other member countries—which many feel are not comparable to German brands—are now allowed to be sold in the country.

EATING OUT

It is easy to find good food in Germany. Restaurants, taverns, and beer gardens all offer delicious food. Generally, the menu is displayed in a box outside at the entrance. For a cheap meal, middle-class Germans can go to Italian, Spanish, Greek or Turkish, and Yugoslav restaurants, while expensive French food is becoming increasingly popular among the upper class. There are also many cake shops and fast food restaurants. Budget meals are also available at some butchers' shops and department stores.

People in Hamburg love to take a break by going to a sidewalk café to eat ice cream and drink something cold.

ALCOHOL

Germany produces much of its own wine, generally in the Rhineland area. Eighty percent of German wine is white, of which much is sweet—like wine from the Rhine Hesse region or the Moselle valley, for instance—and is often drunk after a meal rather than with the food.

A barrel of St. Goarshausen wine.

Wines are categorized into table wines, quality wines, and prime quality wines, and priced accordingly. There are also young wines—like the *Fruhwein* ("Froo-vine") or the *Federwein* ("FAY-der-vine")—and sparkling wines, like *Seckt* ("SEKT"). Wine is not taxed in Germany.

Beer is not only one of Germany's favorite drinks but also a major industry. Germany has about 1,600 breweries and is the second largest brewer of beer in the world after the United States.

Germans drink more beer per head—about 35 gallons per person in 1988—than any other nation.

Hops is grown around Munich, and 90% of the water used in the brewing process comes from wells and springs. Famous German beers include Löwenbrau and Henniger. Many of the local brews from the small breweries in southern Germany are excellent too.

Other popular alcoholic drinks, including the fiery schnapps, are often drunk before a beer and are popular on the cold ski slopes. There are now strict laws concerning the brewing of schnapps in homes in order to control the high alcohol content.

Some popular schnapps include the fruity *Obstler* ("OBST-ler") from south Germany, and the *Korn*, which is a north German grain-based spirit, often with juniper added. *Appelwoi* ("APP-el-voy") is another type which is a hard cider from Hesse.

GERMANY

North Sea

Baltic Sea

Kiel Canal • Kiel

• Hamburg

• Bremen

Netherlands

Weser

Elbe

• Hanover

• Berlin

Poland

• Magdeburg

Duisburg• •Dortmund
Dusseldorf• •Essen

•Cologne

• Leipzig

Belgium

Rhine

• Dresden

Luxembourg

•Frankfurt

Czechoslovakia

•Mannheim

•Nurnberg

France

•Stuttgart

•Munich

Constance

Chiemsee

▲
Zugspitze

Austria

Switzerland

N
↑

Austria D5

Baltic Sea D1
Belgium A3
Berlin D2
Bremen B2

Chiemsee C4
Cologne A3
Constance B5
Czechoslovakia D4

Dortmund A2
Dresden D3
Duisburg A2
Düsseldorf A2

Elbe River C2
Essen A2

France A4
Frankfurt B3

Hamburg B1
Hanover B2

Kiel C1
Kiel Canal B1

Leipzig C3
Luxembourg A3

Magdeburg C2
Mannheim B3
Munich C4

Netherlands A2
North Sea A1
Nurnberg C4

Poland D2

Rhine River A3

Stuttgart B4
Switzerland A5

Weser River B2

Zugspitze C5

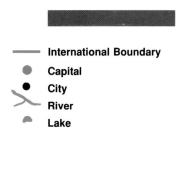

- International Boundary
- Capital
- City
- River
- Lake

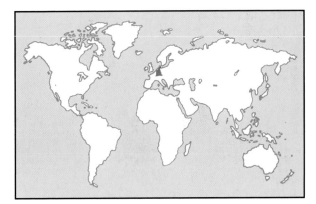

QUICK NOTES

AREA
137,852 square miles

POPULATION
82 million

CAPITAL
Berlin

OFFICIAL LANGUAGE
German

NATIONAL ANTHEM
Einigkeit und Recht und Freiheit ("Unity, justice and freedom")

NATIONAL FLAG
Three horizontal bands—black, red, yellow.

DIFFERENT STATES
Schleswig-Holstein, Lower Saxony, North Rhine-Westphalia, Rhineland-Palatinate, Hesse, Saarland, Baden-Württemberg, Bavaria, Hamburg, Bremen, Berlin, Brandenburg, Mecklenburg-Vorpommern, Saxony, Thuringia, Saxony-Anhalt

MAJOR RELIGION
Christianity

HIGHEST POINT
Zugspitze (9,725 feet)

MAJOR RIVERS
Rhine, Oder, Weser, Elbe and Danube

MAJOR LAKE
Constance

CURRENCY
Deutschmark: 100 pfennings make 1 Deutschmark
(US$1 = DM 1.68)

MAIN EXPORTS
Chemical products, machinery, vehicles, precision and optical goods, office equipment, electrical goods

LEADERS IN THE ARTS
Albrecht Dürer (1471-1528)
Johann Sebastian Bach (1685-1750)
George Handel (1685-1759)
Johann Wolfgang von Goethe (1749–1823)
Friedrich Schiller (1759–1805)
Ludwig van Beethoven (1770-1827)
Thomas Mann (1875–1955)
Hermann Hesse (1877-1962)
Walter Gropius (1883-1969)
Bertolt Brecht (1898–1956)
Günter Grass (b. 1927)
Werner Herzog (b. 1942)

LEADERS IN POLITICS
Konrad Adenauer (chancellor of West Germany 1949–1963)
Willy Brandt (chancellor of West Germany 1969–1974)
Helmut Kohl (chancellor of West Germany 1982–1990; chancellor of reunited Germany 1990 to present)
Erich Honecker (leader of East German SED 1971–1990)

IMPORTANT ANNIVERSARY
Reunification of East and West Germany (October 3)

GLOSSARY

angst	Deep soul searching feeling of guilt, self blame and anxiety.
Basic Law	The fundamental law passed in West Germany after 1945 as a temporary stop gap until eventual reunification with East Germany. The law remains in force today.
Bund	The central, federal government.
Bundestag	The federal parliament.
Gastarbeiter	Immigrant worker.
Land	Individual state within Germany, with its own parliament and set of responsibilities.
Landesrat	A state parliament.
Ostpolitik	Policy of reconciliation with East Germany launched by West German Chancellor Willy Brandt.
Tolle Tage	The crazy days just before Lent when Carnival is at its height.
Wirtschaftswunder	The economic miracle that West Germany experienced during the 1950s.

BIBLIOGRAPHY

Ardagh, John. *Germany and the Germans: An Anatomy of Society Today*, Hamish Hamilton, London, 1987.

Browning, Robert. *The Pied Piper of Hamelin*, Lothrop, New York, 1986.

Craig, Gorden A. *The Germans*, Pelican, London, 1982.

Digens, T. *The Visit*, Viking, New York, 1982.

Shirer, William L. *The Rise and Fall of Adolf Hitler*, Random House, New York, 1963.

Wightman, Margaret. *Faces of Germany*, Harrap, London, 1971.

INDEX

PICTURE CREDITS

Allgemeiner Deutscher Nachrichtendienst: 25, 34, 41, 43, 44, 53, 56, 59, 66, 67, 69, 71, 72, 73, 76, 78, 82, 87, 93, 97, 105.
Victor Englebert: 12, 51, 77, 91, 101, 102, 109, 111, 114, 122.
Life File Photo Library: 4, 15, 22, 24, 49, 68, 100, 104, 117, 119, 120, 123.
The Image Bank: 1, 5, 6, 7, 8, 9, 10, 11, 13, 14, 16, 17, 18, 19, 20, 21, 23, 29, 33, 35, 36, 37, 38, 39, 40, 42, 45, 46, 47, 48, 50, 54, 55, 57, 58, 60, 61, 62, 63, 64, 65, 70, 74, 75, 80, 81, 85, 88, 89, 95, 99, 107, 108, 110, 112, 113, 118, 121, 125.
Sachsische Landesbibliothek: 26, 27, 28, 31, 98.

REFERENCE

7911

WARWICK
KEYS TO HISTORY

The
ARMADA

MARY CONNATTY

Illustrated by
Richard Hook,
Richard Scollins,
Tony Bryant and
Malcolm Porter

Warwick Press
New York/London/Toronto/Sydney
1987

Contents

Published in 1987 by Warwick Press,
387 Park Avenue South, New York, N.Y. 10016.
First published in 1987 by Kingfisher
Books Limited, a Grisewood & Dempsey Company.
Copyright © Grisewood & Dempsey Limited 1987.

6 5 4 3 2 1

Printed in Italy

Library of Congress Catalog Card No.87-50745
ISBN 0-531-19030-7

Author's Note
All dates given in this book are according to the Gregorian or New Style Calendar, announced by Pope Gregory XIII in 1582. Almost all Europe was using the Gregorian Calendar by 1587.

England continued to use the Old Style (Julian) Calendar until 1751, so until this date English documents are according to the Old Style.

The Old Style (Julian) Calendar, devised by Julius Caesar in 46 B.C., took as the length of the lunar year 365 days, 5 hours, 48 minutes, and 46 seconds.

By the sixteenth century the discrepancy amounted to ten days, so, for us today, the English usage of the Julian Calendar gives an incorrect reading of time and weather.

I have chosen the New Style or Gregorian because we use it today and because it corresponds with the actual time and weather conditions of the voyage and battles of the Armada.

Introduction

In the summer of 1588, King Philip II of Spain sent the Great Armada, or armed fleet, to conquer England. This book tells the story of that "great enterprise." It describes the events that led up to the despatch of the Armada, beginning with the developing conflict between England and Spain over the previous century. The story unfolds as the European sea powers battled for world supremacy in religion, trade, and territory.

Philip II had several reasons for grievance where England was concerned. Religion was of prime importance. Sixteenth-century Europe was torn apart by the split between Catholics and Protestants. Henry VIII rejected the power of the Pope and made himself head of the Church in England. Spain remained Catholic and the fanatically religious Philip wanted to make England return to the old faith.

The second important reason was competition for supremacy in trade and sea power. Spain's discovery of the New World opened up a huge source of trade, of which the English wanted a share. The growing expertise of English naval power was a threat to Spain's domination of the seas. Of crucial importance was England's strategic position. With England in his grasp, Philip could command the Channel, encircle Spain's old enemy, France, and have easy passage to the Spanish Netherlands.

Philip's decision to send the Armada was not taken lightly. It was an incredible undertaking. We see how plans went wrong, and how ships were at the mercy of the weather.

There is no doubt that, had the Armada succeeded, Philip would have been rid of Queen Elizabeth. As it turned out its failure was to be to Elizabeth's advantage, and she cleverly turned it into a great English victory. When she died, England was established as a great and growing power. For Spain the tide had turned. Though still dominant in Europe, the disaster of the "Invincible" Armada marked the beginning of her decline.

Philip II of Spain and Elizabeth I of England.

1: The Contenders

Dynasties

One hundred years before the Great Armada sailed to England, Henry VII, the first Tudor king, wanted to expand his power through an alliance with Spain. Ferdinand and Isabella of Spain wanted Henry as an ally against France. So they arranged a marriage for their daughter, Catherine of Aragon, with the heir to the English throne, Arthur, Prince of Wales.

In 1501 Arthur, then fourteen, and Catherine, who was two years older, were married. Within six months Arthur died. His younger brother, Henry, was now heir to the throne. In 1509, when he was just eighteen, he became king, as Henry VIII, and married his brother's widow, Catherine. They wanted a son to keep the Tudor dynasty strong and lasting, but sadly only one of their children, Mary, survived.

Then Henry wanted to put aside Catherine and marry again. When the Pope refused to annul his marriage, Henry made himself head of the church, divorced Catherine and married Anne Boleyn, hoping for a son. The Pope and Catholic leaders declared his marriage to Anne illegal, and their daughter, Elizabeth,

The Tudor family symbol was the rose. Henry VII of Lancaster ended the Wars of the Roses by marrying Elizabeth of York. The red rose of Lancaster was linked with the white rose of York to form the Tudor rose.

The lions and castles of Castile were the important symbols of Spain.

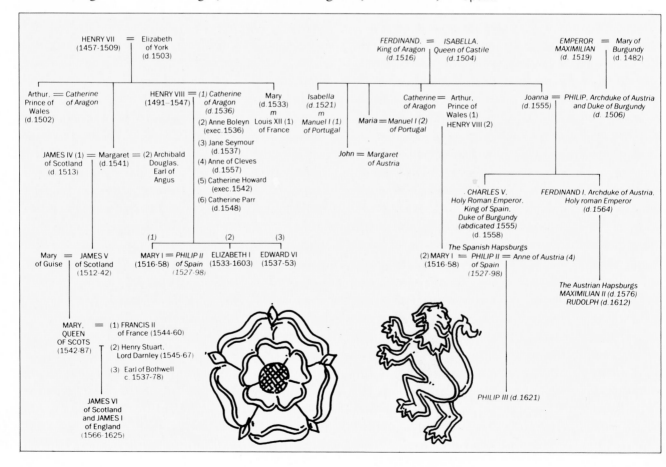

On July 15, 1554 Philip II of Spain and Mary I of England were married in Winchester Cathedral. Royal marriages were arranged, normally by the parents, for reasons of politics, religion, and economics. It was unusual that Mary arranged her own marriage with her cousin, but she was already a queen and 37 years old. Philip was nine years younger and a widower. Both were devout Catholics and wanted to make England Catholic again. Mary very foolishly did not consult many of her advisers, not realizing that Philip's reasons for wanting the marriage were coldly political. But, much to his annoyance, Parliament refused to have him crowned King of England.

illegitimate, with no right to the throne. Henry's divorce from Catherine and his declaration that their daughter, Mary, was a bastard with no right to succeed him, were deep insults to Spain.

In 1536 Henry had Anne Boleyn beheaded for adultery and married his third wife, Jane Seymour. Their son, Edward, became king when Henry died in 1547. During Edward's reign England was strongly Protestant, but he died in 1553 when he was only fifteen and his older half-sister became Queen Mary I.

Mary, the child of Catherine of Aragon, had strong support from Spain. Being half-Spanish, she wanted Spanish friendship and in 1554, she married her cousin, Philip of Spain. His father, Charles V, had counseled him to marry Mary and renew the English–Spanish alliance as a counterbalance against France. Both Philip and Mary thought it their duty to bring England back to Catholicism.

The marriage was unpopular in England because the people hated the Spanish influence. Philip visited England only twice. He was never crowned King of England and did not have power to change English law. However, he involved England in a war with France, in which England lost Calais. This was an immense blow to national prestige, and Mary was blamed. She believed her troubles were God's punishment for the Protestant heresy of her people and increased her drive against Protestants. She had over 300 people burned at the stake for their religious beliefs, earning herself the name "Bloody Mary."

When Mary died in 1558 her Protestant half-sister, Elizabeth, became queen. Philip II, anxious to maintain the alliance, suggested marriage to her. She refused, disliking his strong Catholicism and determined to keep England independent. Tensions increased between England and Spain. The Pope excommunicated Elizabeth in 1570, and she responded by making laws against the Catholics. English Catholics who fled abroad turned to Spain for help to bring the faith back to England. They wanted the Catholic Mary Queen of Scots to be Queen of England. Spain, eager to influence politics and religion in England, supported Mary's claim to the throne.

Elizabeth and Mary, Queen of Scots

Mary, Queen of Scots, was moved from one prison to another in England. Her jailor was the Earl of Shrewsbury, whose wife, the celebrated Bess of Hardwick, spent many hours sewing with Mary.

Before Henry VIII died he made a will stating the succession in the following order: Edward, Mary, and Elizabeth. Most Catholics regarded Elizabeth as illegitimate, with no right to succeed. When Mary died in 1558, Elizabeth became queen and her right was challenged by Catholics who supported Mary, Queen of Scots, who had a claim to the English throne because her grandmother was Henry VIII's sister.

Mary became Queen of the Scots in 1542 when she was a tiny baby. When she was six she was taken to France for her safety. She was brought up a Catholic and treated as a queen in the grand manner of the French court. At sixteen she married the heir to the French throne, who became Francis II a year later. The following year Francis died and, at 17, Mary was a widow. She returned to Scotland in 1561, and her presence there was a great threat to Elizabeth.

While Mary was in France, her mother, the French Mary of Guise, ruled in her place. This gave France immense power over affairs in Scotland, which was resented by many Scottish nobles. A great number of them supported the new Protestant religion. Mary at first took a moderate line with the different religious groups, as Elizabeth was trying to do in England, but English Catholics were commanded by the Pope not to recognize Elizabeth as their queen. She responded by outlawing the practice

of the Catholic faith. Many English Catholics who wished to have Elizabeth as their queen were put in a very difficult position.

In Scotland, Mary married her cousin, Lord Darnley, who also had a claim to the English throne. To begin with, this marriage was supported by Catholics. They had one son, James. His birth strengthened her position, but Darnley was weak and ambitious, and they quarreled bitterly. When Darnley was murdered in 1567, it was thought that Mary was involved in the plot. People became more suspicious when she married the Earl of Bothwell, who was certainly involved in Darnley's murder. Mary was forced off the throne, and her infant son became James VI of Scotland. Mary fled south, hoping Elizabeth would help her regain the Scottish throne. It was a wild dream.

Mary became one of Elizabeth's greatest problems. If she allowed Mary to go free, Catholics would have access to her and the opportunity to dethrone Elizabeth. Mary was imprisoned and, for eighteen years while Elizabeth's followers wanted to get rid of her, Catholics plotted against Elizabeth.

The Pope, Philip II of Spain, and English Catholics in exile were all involved in efforts to free Mary to establish her as Queen of Scotland and make her Queen of England. Most of these plots were made abroad and came to nothing. In 1586 a more serious affair occurred. Anthony Babington, a young gentleman from Derbyshire, conspired to free Mary, to "despatch the usurping Competitor" (Elizabeth) and put Mary on the throne. The plot was discovered; Babington and his friends were condemned to be hanged, drawn, and quartered. Mary was tried and executed.

Mary's execution shocked Europe. Catholics looked upon her as a martyr. Philip II felt obliged to avenge her death. At the same time, Mary's death left him free to claim the English throne.

Elizabeth was very reluctant to have Mary, Queen of Scots, put to death. Mary was her cousin and of royal blood. But Mary's presence in England was a great stumbling block to peace. Many powerful Catholics supported her, but Protestant nobles wanted her out of the way. Their opportunity came with the discovery of the Babington Plot. Mary was involved and tried for treason and found guilty. Elizabeth delayed signing the death warrant, but she did so at last on January 22, 1587. The sentence was carried out quickly and Mary went to her execution with great courage. Here she is being brought to her execution and prepared for her beheading. In contrast to the wretchedness of her imprisonment, Mary was given a grand state funeral at Peterborough Cathedral. In 1612 her son, James I, had her coffin removed to Westminster Abbey in London, where it lies beneath a sumptuous white marble monument.

The Growth of Power in Tudor England

Henry VII, the first Tudor monarch, was determined to expand his riches and power by increasing trade. England was then an agricultural country with a population of about 3,000,000. English merchants grew rich from the export of woolen cloth, and the King filled his treasury from the customs duty charged on the exports. The Merchant Adventurers of London dominated the wool trade, and Antwerp in the Netherlands was the great port through which English merchandise entered Europe.

A shortage of English ships forced merchants to ship their goods in foreign vessels, such as those of the Hanseatic League, which had depots in England and in the ports of northern Europe. Henry VII introduced Navigation Acts in 1485 and 1489 to encourage English merchants to build their own ships to carry their own merchandise. He also took steps to extend trade in Europe by making agreements with France, Portugal, and Spain.

Competition was fierce between trading states. When the English began to buy wine, dried fruit, and spices from Crete and Middle Eastern countries, they came up against the merchants of Venice, who monopolized trade in the Mediterranean. Henry retaliated by making a treaty with Florence, using the port of Pisa as a depot for English wool.

In 1496 Henry sent John Cabot to explore the east coast of North America, and his discoveries led to the formation of a Bristol company, the Adventurers of the New Found Lands, to extend English trade across the Atlantic.

In Henry VIII's reign the wool trade continued to flourish, but he was more intent on territorial gain than his father. England still

Henry VIII spent lavishly on entertainments and pageants. He loved music and feasting and employed many artists to decorate his great palaces. As a young man he was tall and splendidly athletic, with golden hair and glowing skin. He lived too well and his huge suit of armor in the Tower of London shows his enormous size in old age.

The proudest ship of Henry VIII's navy was the *Henry Grace à Dieu*, nicknamed *Great Harry*. It was launched at Woolwich in 1514, a huge, high-built, ship, weighing 1,500 tons and carrying 184 guns and a crew of 700. Later, in the time of Henry's daughter, Elizabeth I, warships became lower, leaner, and swifter.

owned Calais and a piece of surrounding territory, and Henry was eager to extend his power into France. He made two attempts to regain French territory and had great battleships like the *Henri Grace à Dieu* and the *Mary Rose* built for that purpose. He also had a series of forts, blockhouses, and castles erected along the south coast. These were later reinforced by Elizabeth as defense against the Spaniards.

When Mary I was queen she lost Calais to the French, but exploration for trade routes was renewed. In 1554 Richard Chancellor sailed northeast to Archangel to open up trade with Russia. He visited Moscow and was received at the court of Ivan the Terrible.

After Mary died and Elizabeth became queen, England entered the competition for world markets. Elizabeth employed the experienced John Hawkins to build up her navy. At that time there was little difference between merchant and fighting ships, because merchant vessels carried arms for defense against pirates, and in times of war they could easily be converted into battleships. English ships were designed to be faster than the Spanish, and, though England and Spain were officially at peace, English ships attacked Spanish treasure ships returning from the New World. This further increased the growing tension between the two countries.

One of the toughest competitors to the English was the Hanseatic League, a group of German merchants who dominated the Baltic and north European trade. The Hanseatic League had bases like this one in London.

2: Background to History

The Age of Discovery

The sixteenth century was a period of great expansion for Europe. The known world, which had until then been only Europe, Asia, and Africa, was opened up by the new great voyages of discovery.

In 1492 Ferdinand and Isabella of Spain sent Christopher Columbus in command of three small ships to find a western route to Asia. After two months at sea Columbus sighted land and thought he had reached the eastern coast of Asia. He was wrong.

He had discovered islands of a new world unknown to Europeans. The first island that Columbus came to was probably San Salvador in the Bahamas. Weeks later he reached Cuba and Haiti. He called these islands the West Indies. On his three further voyages he discovered more islands and the mainland of South America and Central America. Until his death he believed that these lands previously unknown to Europe were a part of Asia. Soon other adventurers were following excitedly in the footsteps of Columbus or seeking other new lands.

In 1497 Vasco da Gama, a Portuguese, rounded the Cape of Good Hope and sailed up the coast of East Africa and across the Indian Ocean to Goa on the coast of India.

The Spanish continued to look for a route to Asia across the Atlantic and eventually, in 1520, Ferdinand Magellan found the route by sailing around the tip of South America, through the strait which was to be named after him, and then out into the

The map shows the routes of the great explorers. Portugal was more interested in trade than settlement. For Spain, with her huge population, America was an outlet for adventurous men and women, eager to get rich. Both countries wanted riches, but the conversion of the heathen to Christianity was equally important. But often human greed was stronger than the desire to convert the pagans, who were reduced to slavery.

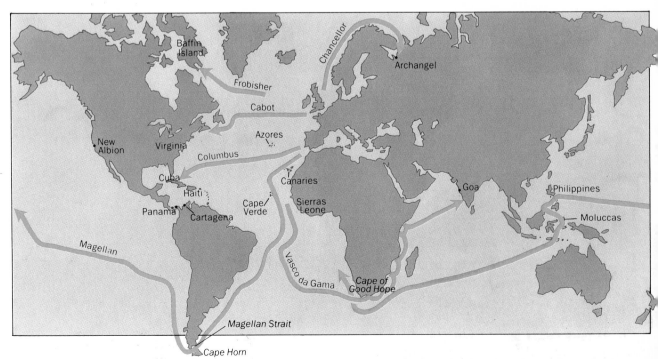

This early map of South America and the Strait of Magellan shows how little was known of the geography of the New World. Imaginary animals inhabit the land, and on the tree hangs the coat-of-arms of Spain.

In 1519, Ferdinand Magellan, a Portuguese paid by the Spanish, set sail westward to find a passage to the Spice Islands. He found a way around the tip of South America through the strait now named after him. It is 350 miles long with high cliffs making a wind tunnel that creates appalling storms. In 1521 when Magellan sailed out of the strait into calm water he named the new sea the Pacific (or peaceful) ocean. He was killed later in the Philippines, but his fleet reached Spain the following year, to complete the first round the world voyage.

When the Spanish first discovered Central and South America they made friends with the natives, but when they needed labor for their plantations and mines, they forced the natives to work. As more laborers were needed, slaves were brought by traders from the west of Africa. Before the trade was stopped in the nineteenth century, over 10,000,000 slaves had been taken to the Americas.

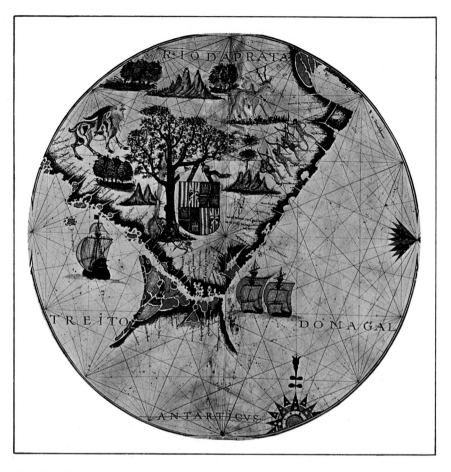

Pacific Ocean. Magellan was killed in the Philippines, but one of his ships reached Spain in 1522, having completed the first round the world voyage.

In 1576 Martin Frobisher, a tough Yorkshireman, reached Baffin Island, and one year later Francis Drake set out on the three-year journey that made him the first Englishman to circumnavigate the world.

When the Spanish discovered gold and silver in Mexico and Peru other European seafaring nations were eager to take part in the trade, but Spain, first on the scene in the New World, was unwilling to share her wealth.

World trade was now taking over from European trade, but for the English the slave trade off the coast of West Africa was a profitable source of wealth. The Spanish settlers in the West Indies and South America needed labor badly on their plantations and in the silver mines, and John Hawkins and others provided this "merchandise."

After 1580, when Philip II annexed Portugal, Spanish territories in the New World stretched from the basin of the Mississippi River in North America down to the mouth of the Rio de la Plata in Argentina. Spain became the undisputed Catholic power in the world, to whom the Pope looked for religious zeal and political support.

Spain and her Allies

Ferdinand and Isabella of Spain had greatly expanded their power, through marriage alliances and by expansion into the New World. Their grandson, Emperor Charles V, split these vast territories between his brother and his son Philip. In 1556 Philip became King Philip II of Spain, the Spanish Netherlands, and King of the Two Sicilies. With the land owned by Spain in the Americas, he ruled the largest kingdom in Christendom.

His marriage to Mary Tudor was intended to extend Spanish power into England, but Mary's death brought this alliance to an end. Philip wanted to dominate England, but he had wanted to do it peacefully, and he did not, in any case, have enough money to make war at that time.

From 1580 the immense influx of silver into Spain from Peru and Mexico encouraged Philip to expand his power. In 1580 he took Portugal and Spanish troops attacked Smerwick Harbour in Ireland. The English commander slaughtered most of the Spanish garrison after their surrender, and this deepened the tension.

Before Mary, Queen of Scots was executed in 1587, she named Philip as her successor to the English throne. This meant that, in the eyes of the Catholic church, he was legal monarch of England. With England in his grasp, Spain would be in a splendid position to send troops to suppress the rebelious Netherlands.

Philip II was an aging man of sixty when he planned the Great Armada. He carried on his work in a simple study deep inside his grand palace of the Escorial near Madrid. To this lonely room came messengers from his ambassadors in London, Paris, and Rome, from Parma in the Netherlands, keeping him informed of English naval strength, of English troops in the Netherlands and of the activities of Catholic exiles in Rome. The information was often misleading and, in the gloomy isolation of his palace, he became gradually out of touch with the world. The failure of the Armada was partly due to Philip's lack of contact with his captains. Had he visited the ports and inspected the progress of preparations he would have been aware of the shortcomings of his plans.

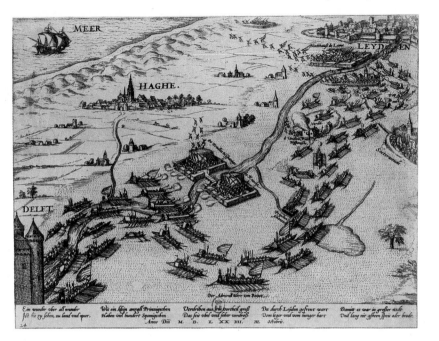

The Sea Beggars were secretly helped by Elizabeth I, who allowed them to shelter in English ports. English volunteers fought alongside the Dutch against the Spanish troops in the Netherlands, and Dutch refugees flocked into England. Justin of Nassau, Admiral of Zeeland, a son of William the Silent, patrolled the shallow waters off the Dutch coast with his flat-bottomed fly boats. Parma's crack troops had little hope of embarking from Neeuport or Dunkirk with Nassau lying in wait.

Troubles in the Spanish Netherlands

The Netherlands was made up of a number of rich and densely populated provinces under Spanish rule. In 1566, the tyrannical rule of Philip II had reached such a pitch that the Dutch people rose in rebellion. Philip, who ruled from faraway Madrid, sent the harsh Duke of Alva to suppress the rebellion and enforce the Catholic faith. This hardened the revolt.

A group of Protestant noblemen, headed by William the Silent, formed a petition to ask for certain rights. They were laughed at as "Beggars" by the Spanish. Furious at such treatment, they formed their own fleet and organized raids on Spanish shipping in the English Channel and North Sea, and proudly called themselves the "Sea Beggars." William the Silent tried to keep the Netherlands united, but the northern states broke away and became Protestant. William was assassinated in 1584, but his son, Maurice, carried on the revolt.

Officially England and Spain were then at peace. Spanish ships used English ports until a huge shipment of silver was confiscated at Southampton by order of Elizabeth. The Duke of Alva was furious and stopped trade with England.

In 1578 Philip sent the Duke of Parma to win back the Protestants in the Netherlands. Parma's successes were cut short by Philip's plans to invade England.

Philip's great scheme was to sail up the English Channel with a huge force and escort Parma's army across to England. Once on English soil, Parma's expert military leadership and experienced soldiers would play a large part in the conquest of England. The success of the Armada depended on this link up with Parma.

William von Lumey, commander of the Sea Beggars, vowed that he would not cut his hair or his nails until he defeated the Spaniards.

The Great English Sea Captains

Elizabeth I was well aware that England's greatness as a world power depended on a strong seagoing force. Such a force would enable the English to establish valuable trading routes, to spread her influence abroad, and to defend her shores. Elizabeth therefore greatly prized her sea captains. The most famous and favored were cousins: Francis Drake and John Hawkins.

After childhood poverty, living with his family near Chatham in Kent in the hull of a ship, Drake was apprenticed to the master of a ship trading with the northern European ports. He came to know every current and sandbank of the English Channel and the North Sea. When the ship's master died, he left his vessel to Drake, who, like many young sailors of his time, sought his fortune in trade with the New World. His first trip there was with his cousin, John Hawkins, who had a thriving trade in slaves from West Africa to the Spanish settlements in the West Indies and Central America. Hawkins and the Spaniards were breaking the law, for Philip II forbade foreign ships to enter Spanish ports abroad, but the Spaniards needed goods, and slaves to work for them. Hawkins also attacked Spanish treasure ships on their way home from the New World. This was open piracy, but Elizabeth turned a blind eye to it, often sharing in the profits.

In 1567 she even lent two ships to Hawkins when he and Drake went on a slaving expedition. When they had sold most of their cargo, the Spanish ambushed them, sinking all but two of their ships and capturing about 400 men. Drake escaped in the *Judith*; Hawkins followed in the tiny *Minion*. Three months later Drake's battered ship, full of starving and dying men, limped into Plymouth Sound. A month later Hawkins arrived, in even worse condition.

Hawkins now gave up his seafaring career and became Comptroller of the Navy. Drake continued to harrass the Spaniards, growing rich on the spoils and supported by the Queen, which deeply offended the Spanish. In 1577 he set sail on the greatest voyage of his career, the circumnavigation of the world. He followed Magellan's route around Cape Horn. Here storms broke up his fleet, but Drake carried on alone in the *Golden Hinde* to capture Spanish treasure ships off the west coast of South America. He then set off across the unknown Pacific, onward through the Indian Ocean and around the Cape of Good Hope toward home. On September 26, 1580 he sailed his little ship into Plymouth. For this achievement, Queen Elizabeth knighted Drake.

Then in 1586 Drake led a fleet to Cadiz to destroy Spanish ships. This was the famous "singeing of the King's beard." The havoc caused delayed the Armada by six months. The Spaniards had to make new casks and barrels with unseasoned wood, which soured their water and rotted their food on the voyage of the Armada.

The Spaniards called Sir Francis Drake "Il Draco," the Dragon, and many thought he had a magic mirror in his ship's cabin which helped him to find Spanish treasure convoys.

John Hawkins's knowledge of ships and navigation were invaluable to Elizabeth I. As Comptroller of her navy, he built new ships, lower, longer, and easier to sail.

In February 1586 Drake set out from Plymouth with ships supplied by the Queen, the Earl of Leicester, Sir Walter Raleigh, and others. His aim was to take revenge in the New World for Philip's capture of English corn ships the previous year, in the port of Bilbao. The English swarmed into Cartagena, the capital of Spanish South America, and the inhabitants fled. An English captain wrote, "our pikes were longer than theirs, and our bodies better armed; with which advantage our swords and pikes grew too hard for them and they were driven to give place."

Planning the Invincible Armada

In 1580 Philip II annexed Portugal and added the ships from her splendid navy to the Spanish fleet. Silver from the mines in the New World was bringing in immense wealth. Now Philip, with his Lord High Admiral, Santa Cruz, began to plan the invasion of England, but in 1586 Santa Cruz died and the Duke of Medina Sidonia took his place. He was neither a soldier nor a sailor, but was chosen by Philip as one of the greatest noblemen in Spain. Wisely, he took advice from the experienced commanders.

The execution of Mary, Queen of Scots, by order of Elizabeth, in 1587 shocked all Catholic nations. Named by Mary, Queen of Scots, as her successor, Philip was ready now to establish himself as the rightful King of England. He ordered the Duke of Medina to prepare the great fleet to sail up the English Channel to link up with Parma's army from the Netherlands. Together they would invade England.

The organization of the "Great Enterprise" was a colossal task. Philip sent agents to Germany and Italy to buy cannon, armor, gunpowder, shot, swords, and all the weapons of war. He chartered vessels from many European nations.

The main task of the Armada would be to transport soldiers to fight in England. Apart from the 22 great Portuguese and Spanish fighting galleons, there were merchant ships converted for battle. Smaller panaches and zabras were used as messenger ships and also for picket or guard duty.

The great unwieldy, lumbering urcas carried siege guns and equipment intended for land battles. They were filled to bursting point with guns, horses, mules, and ammunition.

Collecting the stores and equipment for the Great Armada was a prodigious task. Enough food had to be supplied for six months. Eleven million pounds of biscuit, 600,000 pounds of salt pork, 40,000 gallons of olive oil, 14,000 barrels of wine were but a part of the necessities for a force of over 30,000 men. The great transport urcas were to be filled with 5,000 extra pairs of shoes, 11,000 pairs of sandals, as well as equipment to repair ships, and axes, spades, and shovels for digging trenches and sieges.

With the fleet went six surgeons and six physicians, 180 priests as spiritual advisers, 19 justices and 50 administrators, carefully selected to set up government in England, and 146 young gallants who volunteered for the adventure, and took with them 728 servants.

The Armada was divided into ten squadrons, led by the most famous and experienced commanders of the Spanish forces. In charge of the Biscay ships was Don Juan Martinez de Recalde. Don Pedro de Valdes led the Andalusian ships. Don Miguel de Oquendo, nicknamed the "Glory of the Fleet," was the heroic leader of the Guipuzcoan fleet. One of the most dashing commanders was the young Don Alonso de Leyva, whose task was to take over should Medina be killed or disabled.

The oldest commander was Don Juan Martinez de Recalde who was 62 at the time of the Great Armada.

3: Setting Sail

Key points in England's defenses were the castles of Sandgate, Walmer, Deal, and Dover. Deal Castle, built by Henry VIII in 1539–40, was restored in the 1580s. It is typical of the massive, squat fortifications of Henry's time. Its enormously thick walls and rounded bastions were designed to deflect gunshot (see below). Other work was done in restoring Dover pier, adding a stone quay and gun platform to Portsmouth, and renewing defenses on the Isle of Wight, at Southampton, Brownsea Island, Portland, Plymouth, and at Pendennis Castle and St. Mawes in Cornwall.

The Defense of England

With the renewed threat from Spain in the 1580s, England had begun to step up her defenses. The attack was expected from the south, so all along the coast from Cornwall to the mouth of the Thames the castles, forts, and blockhouses of Henry VIII's time were restored. The prime target of Philip II's troops must be the capture of London, so its defenses were of the utmost importance.

The blockhouses at East Mersea and West Tilbury were repaired and Queenborough Castle on the Isle of Sheppey was reinforced to protect London. The only new fort built in Elizabeth's reign was at Upnor on the Medway, especially designed to guard the new naval dockyard at Chatham.

There was no standing army in England so armed bands or militia were organized locally. The Queen's great favorite, Robert Dudley, Earl of Leicester, was given the important task of defending London and the Queen. Leicester had his main force at Tilbury. He had led a force against the experienced troops of

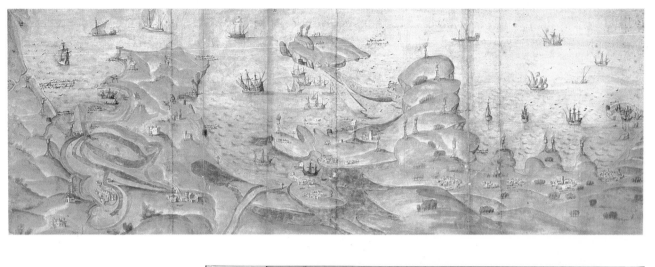

Fortifications

Parma, so he knew what to expect. Farther inland the gentry were slow to raise armed bands. Being so far from the coast, they felt little danger.

Most important was the organization of the navy. John Hawkins had been hard at work designing new ships. Francis Drake created a new method of fighting. The traditional style of sea battle was for ships to come within close range of each other, grappling irons were slung from ship to ship, soldiers swung themselves onto the enemy ships and fought hand-to-hand. The ships were built with high fore and aft castles which were defended like castles on land.

Drake changed this method completely. He trained his sailors to fight by handling their ships expertly, and, by using long range guns, they could out-gun and out-maneuver the enemy.

John Hawkins's new English ships went into battle "line ahead," or one following the other, sailing past the enemy while firing lethal broadsides into their ships.

The Spanish had been ordered, should they engage the English ships, to bear down on them and use the old style of grappling and boarding, but the faster English vessels with their long range guns kept out of range. The battles of the Armada were the first in which the English used this method of fighting. From that time it became the normal style of encounter in sea battles.

A network of beacons was constructed on headlands and hills. It stretched like a monster cobweb across the counties of southern England. Men were posted, two by day and two by night, to light the beacons. The glow from these great bonfires could be seen across the country, signaling the arrival of the Great Armada.

The placing of warning beacons on high ground was common practice when invasion was expected in England. In 1588 almost every parish in southern England had one. Sadly, many parish records have vanished, but sites of Armada beacons are still known, the most famous being St. Michael's Mount in Cornwall. Black Down, near Haslemere, was another ancient beacon restored in Elizabethan times. Near Brighton, Ditchling Beacon stands on the site of an ancient hill fort.

Both English and Spanish ships varied enormously in size. A great galleass, such as the *Girona* which sank off the Giant's Causeway in Ireland, could be 160 feet long, about the length of six buses. The galleass was a combination of galley and galleon, with both oars and sails. It was a cumbersome vessel against the new English "race" ships. The *Golden Hinde*, at 70 feet, was half the length of a Spanish galleass.

Even so, the great English ships, the *Ark Royal*, the *Revenge*, the *Nonpareil*, towered above the fishing boats that put out from the south coast ports to their aid during the battles. Even before England became Protestant, her ships were given names like *Dreadnought*, *Swiftsure*, *Tiger*, *Triumph*, while Spain preferred saints' names, such as *San Martin*, *San Lorenzo* and *Rata Santa Maria Encoronada*.

The Spanish ships (above) remained heavy and more unwieldy, designed for the old style of fighting from ship to ship rather as if they were floating castles.

John Hawkins built new ships specially designed for Francis Drake's newly created type of sea battle. He also remade the old ones by cutting off the high castles. Sometimes he even had them lengthened by cutting the ships in half and inserting whole new sections. These longer, lower ships

(below) lay snug in the water and were much easier to manage. They were called "race" ships, not because they were fast, but because the high castles had been "razed" or cut down. Being longer, they could also carry a greater number of cannon.

War and Weapons

By the sixteenth century, gunpowder was in common use. Its immense power meant that siege warfare had become a highly technical science. The Italians were experts in the arts of war, and the Earl of Leicester employed several to design his defenses. Frederico Giambelli made the defenses at Tilbury strong enough to withstand the siege guns of the Spanish.

Both English and Spanish soldiers used muskets and arquebuses. Bows and arrows were still in use, and the English were famous for their expertise with the longbow. The sixteenth-century long pike, with its vicious iron point, was a lethal weapon against cavalry. Pikemen had to be fast and strong, to handle the long pike which stood about three times the height of a man. Their battle tactic was to form tight squares, with pikes held aloft, like hedgehogs. When the enemy cavalry charged, down came the pikes like a fearsome metal hedge. Halberds, the sixteenth century version of the poleax, were nasty weapons for hand-to-hand fighting. They were very heavy, so the halberdiers had to be extremely strong men.

Foot soldiers, such as pikemen, bowmen, halberdiers, musketeers, and arquebusiers all wore some form of metal armor, and their only uniform was a bright tabard or tunic to show their squadron or army.

On board ship the gun crews worked in such hot, cramped conditions that they were usually stripped to the waist, with handkerchiefs tied around their heads to keep the sweat out of their eyes. They were unable to stand upright between the low decks. In battle the gun decks were an appalling combination of noise, heat, smoke, and confusion.

The Spanish foot soldier wore a "morion" or helmet. His body was protected by half armor or corselet.

Two main types of cannon were used in the battles of the Armada. One was cast in a single piece of bronze and loaded from the muzzle (below). The other (right) was made on the principle of a wooden barrel with wrought-iron staves or strips and hoops welded together. It had a detachable powder chamber or breech piece.

The Armada Sails

On May 11, 1588, the Great Armada set sail from Lisbon. For days the fleet had been waiting for a favorable wind. On board his flagship, the *San Martin*, the Duke of Medina ordered a great cannon to be fired as the tide turned and a light wind came up from the east. Then the deep sound of bugles across the water signaled the ships to weigh anchor and make sail. A colossal din broke out as sailors hauled in cables and hoisted sails. At last, the great adventure had begun.

Like a magnificent royal pageant the ships sailed in stately procession down river to the sea, their colorful squadron banners fluttering in the breeze, following in the wake of Medina's flagship, which flew the brilliant royal standard of Spain. Blessed by their priests, 130 ships carrying 30,000 men were setting out to conquer England.

However, sailing ships are at the mercy of the weather. Before the fleet reached open water, the wind changed to a strong north-west; the Great Armada was forced to anchor and shelter at the mouth of the Tagus. In the heavy swell, the Duke of Medina, like many of his sailors, became very seasick.

For over two weeks the suffering crews waited and then set sail once more. In heavy seas, through day and night, it was impossible to stay together. After three weeks, storms forced the fleet to seek shelter in Corunna. Here Medina waited for the scattered ships to assemble.

With rotting food, stinking water, and many sick, it seemed foolish to go on, but Philip II insisted. A month later, with fresh supplies and ships repaired as best they could, the Great Armada set off again. This time they were lucky. The wind that took them north, blew back the English fleet that had sailed out from Plymouth to stop them.

On Friday, July 29 Captain Thomas Flemyng in the *Golden Hinde* put into Plymouth to say he had sighted the Armada off the Lizard 50 miles away.

England in Wait

In the sixteenth century it was the custom for the aristocracy to command. Queen Elizabeth appointed as Lord Admiral and Commander-in-Chief of her navy, her cousin, Lord Howard of Effingham. Lord Howard's father, two uncles, and great grandfather had been Lords Admirals, so he had the sea in his blood. Philip II had also chosen a great noble, the Duke of Medina Sidonia, to lead the Armada.

Howard wisely appointed as his second-in-command the experienced Sir Francis Drake, who was a superb leader, with a deep knowledge of the sea, loved and admired by his sailors. He commanded the 500-ton *Revenge*, rebuilt to John Hawkins's design. Other famous sea captains in the Plymouth Squadron were Thomas Fenner, Martin Frobisher, and Edward Fenton. John Hawkins was in charge of the Medway Squadron, and Lord Henry Seymour guarded the Dover Strait. The Queen's navy now consisted of 47 fighting ships. To these were added ships volunteered by gentry and noblemen at their own expense.

Peace Negotiations

Even as the Great Armada was sailing north, peace talks continued between Elizabeth and the Duke of Parma. The revolt in the Spanish Netherlands had dragged on from 1566, leaving the country in a state of chaos. By 1579, William the Silent, leader of the Protestants, was convinced that Spain would never give them freedom of religion or government.

In 1584, William the Silent was assassinated. The Catholic Duke of Parma grasped the opportunity and began to win back the northern states. In desperation, the Protestant states turned to England for help, but Elizabeth sent only a small army under the Earl of Leicester. It was agreed that two Dutch ports, Flushing and Brill, were to be governed by English commanders.

In August, 1587, Parma captured the important city of Sluys, giving him access to the sea. Leicester's army was unsuccessful and he was recalled, but English troops remained in Holland to help the Protestants. Spies kept Elizabeth informed of the movements and size of Parma's army. Philip II wanted to get the English out of Holland, and this was yet another reason for sending the Great Armada.

The Duke of Parma played for time, keeping Elizabeth's ambassadors talking, while the flyboats of the Protestant Justin of Nassau (William the Silent's son) kept up a blockade of the deep-water Dutch ports. Parma had to prepare Nieuport and Dunkirk from which to launch his ships. These ports were very shallow with shifting sandbanks. Parma expected that the Armada would destroy the English fleet and clear a passage for his barges to cross the Channel and invade England. He pretended to the English that his preparations were for a local campaign.

This confused state of affairs continued until the Armada

Country gentry were required to organize armed bands or militia. Sir Walter Raleigh, a member of Elizabeth's defense committee, was sent to raise armed bands in the West Country. Parishes also raised their own civil defense. An odd assortment of armor and arms were collected: helmets, gauntlets, corselets, and girdles; swords, daggers, halberds, pikes, and muskets. We have no idea of the condition of these arms, but much of it was probably old and rusty, and country folk had only farm tools as weapons.

Why did the Duke of Parma (below), the greatest military leader in Europe, fail to embark his troops? Parma reported that his barges, laden with troops, could only reach England in fine weather, and if escorted by the Armada. He told the King that the big Spanish ships would not find deep anchorage near Dunkirk and that enemy flyboats would prevent him from coming out. Philip never reported this to Medina, who on approaching Dunkirk was appalled to find no safe anchorage.

entered the English Channel and had its first encounter with Elizabeth's navy.

Elizabeth was also playing for time, assembling her fleet and mobilizing her troops. The Spanish War Council had distributed a list of all items of the Armada, including torture instruments: a piece of propaganda intended to terrify the enemy. The Spaniards did not disclose their plan of action and Elizabeth's secret agents had no idea where the Armada would land. The English thought it would be the mouth of the Thames, where Leicester was frantically building defenses at Tilbury and near Gravesend. In fact, the Spanish planned to land near Margate, an area poorly defended by the English. Altogether, the English land defenses were haphazard and unfinished. It was, therefore, of the utmost importance that the navy was powerful enough to prevent the Spaniards from landing.

Elizabeth was cautious. She did not want England to fire the first shot. Drake thought differently. He was convinced the way to beat the Spanish was to attack them in their own ports. When he heard the Armada was halted by storms at Corunna, he persuaded the Queen to let him take a fleet to attack them. But his ships were beaten back by bad weather.

On July 31, near the Eddystone, the Duke of Medina, like a knight of old, hoisted the standard of Spain on the main topmast of his flagship, the *San Martin*. It was the signal to begin the battle. Lord Howard sent the *Disdain* to accept the challenge. Then Howard, in his flagship, the *Ark Royal* led out his squadron in line ahead. The war between England and Spain had begun.

4: Engagement

Encounter

When Sir Francis Drake heard that the Great Armada had been sighted off the Lizard, he was playing bowls on Plymouth Hoe. He made the now legendary comment: "There is plenty of time to finish the game, and beat the Spaniards." In fact, Drake had time to spare. It was low tide, and impossible to take the fleet out of harbor for another eight hours.

When they did set sail with 54 ships, it was raining so hard the fleets could scarcely see each other. In sailing ships the most important tactic in battle is to get to the windward of the enemy. Then a captain can sail his ship into the attack, while his enemy has the wind blowing against him. To get to windward or "win the weather gauge" is vital. The Spaniards admired the ability of the new English ships to win the weather gauge. The English were deeply impressed by the discipline of the Spaniards and how they kept close formation. In this first encounter a few shots were fired, but little damage was done.

So the Armada sailed on, followed by the English. Two great Spanish ships were put out of action by accident. The *Rosario* collided with others and was disabled. At dawn on Sunday, August 1, she was captured by Drake and towed into Torbay. Her commander Don Pedro de Valdes, was taken prisoner. Recalde's *San Salvador* blew up with tremendous loss of life. She was abandoned and the English towed her into Weymouth. Aboard

The course of the Armada from the Lizard to Gravelines a distance of about 279 miles. The Armada was spread out in a great arc, like a huge bird with a seven-mile wingspan. The Duke of Medina led in his flagship, the *San Martin*, with a vanguard of principal battleships. In the center were clustered the slow-moving urcas or transports, closely guarded in the rear by the experienced Recalde with his Biscayan Squadron. On the wings were some of the most powerful galleons.

After the first encounter off the Eddystone, the Spanish changed their battle order and put some of their best warships in the rear to beat off the harrying English.

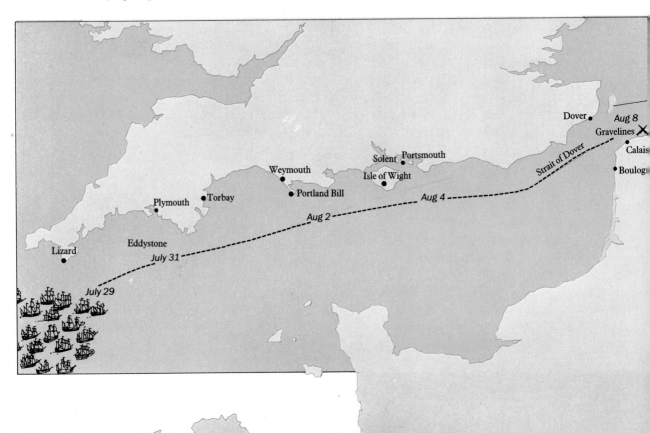

her they found 2,000 cannon balls and 140 barrels of gunpowder, which were quickly taken by the *Golden Hinde* to the main fleet.

On August 2, off Portland Bill the second battle took place. This time the Spanish had the advantage of the weather gauge. At long range little damage was done. The English reported the "waste of a terrible value of shot." The fragile rigging and castles of the Spanish ships were easily penetrated, but not their solid hulls. The Spanish could not get close enough to grapple and board the English vessels.

On August 4, as the Isle of Wight came into view, the Duke of Medina, with the English hard on his heels, had many things on his mind. Ammunition was running low. He had sent messages to Parma, with no response. Now his letters, sent by pinnace, became more urgent, asking for shot.

The English were determined to prevent the Spanish entering the Solent. In calm weather, Howard ordered the *Ark Royal* to be towed into battle by rowboats, followed by the *Golden Lion*. Three Spanish galleasses detached themselves from the fleet to do battle. For hours the great ships pounded each other, watched by their fleets. Then the wind rose to the Spaniards' advantage, but again the nimble English got away. With a southwest wind the Great Armada continued toward the Strait of Dover, in the hope of meeting Parma at Dunkirk. As he sailed, Medina was given the appalling news that there was no anchorage deep enough for the fleet on the Flemish shore.

From the cliffs and shore people watched in amazement at the grand spectacle as the Armada, like a stately pageant of gilded ships, their banners flying, sailed up the Channel. Behind them came the English, equally magnificent, bristling with cannon, their upper decks gleaming with gold carvings and brilliantly colored coats of arms. What were the watchers' feelings? Fear, or pride that the Queen's splendid navy kept the Spanish out to sea? Off the Isle of Wight the boom of heavy guns could be heard as Lord Howard led his ships into the attack to prevent the Spaniards from entering the Solent. Then the Spanish continued on their way; the English ships in hot pursuit.

Fire at Sea

Little damage could be done to the Armada on the move. With the great fleet forced to anchor off Calais it was a different matter. Now was the time to send in fireships. The Spanish knew that the Italian engineer, Giambelli, had made fireships laden with explosives for the English. These "Hellburners" were the most fearful weapons for a fleet at anchor.

The Spanish began to prepare. Pinnaces stood guard with long grapnels to tow the fireships away from the main fleet. Medina ordered the ships to be ready to weigh anchor for a quick getaway. As it was a lengthy business hauling up heavy sea anchors, the tactic was to attach them to buoys. If the fireships came, then the ships cut their cables and escaped, leaving the heavy anchors attached to the buoys. When the danger was over the ships could return to pick up the anchors.

Lord Howard's squadrons were joined by the Dover Squadron, led by Lord Henry Seymour. Now the Queen's navy almost equaled the Armada in number. The English recognized their advantage. They filled eight old ships with inflammable material and waited for the wind and tide.

After midnight, the waiting Spaniards saw the glow from the fireships approaching on the tide. As they came closer, their guns heated and exploded, making a terrifying sight. The Spanish hastily cut their cables. In the pitch darkness they collided with each other in their effort to escape. The huge galleass, the *San Lorenzo*, was badly damaged, but no ship was set on fire.

In "An Engagement between the English and Spanish Fleets," (right) the great galleasses fly the red flag of Spain with a gold cross, while the English fly the white flag of St George with its red cross. Striped flags indicate individual squadrons.

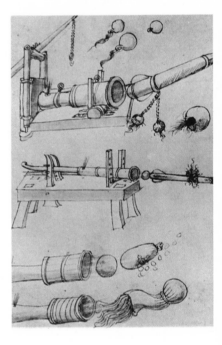

Cannon were loaded from the muzzle end. The gunpowder, wrapped in cloth, was pushed down the barrel, followed by wadding, rammed into place to hold the powder and keep it dry. Then came the shot and a second piece of wadding. At the word of command, the gunner lit his linstock, put it to the touch-hole in the barrel and the gun fired.

This contemporary map tells three stories. The English squadrons sail out from Plymouth. The Armada challenges the English and battle takes place south of the Eddystone rock. The English fleet chases the Armada south of Start Point. The battle formations are imaginary and would have been far less orderly.

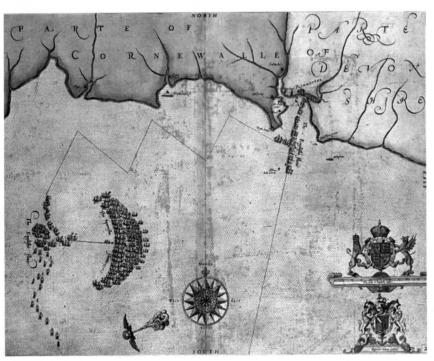

The Battle of Gravelines

At daylight on August 8, Medina realized many of his ships were in danger of running on the shoals of the Flemish coast, an easy target for the pursuing English. With four great ships he decided to stand and fight, desperately determined to hold off the English while the rest of the Armada collected and made ready for the coming assault.

Drake, in the *Revenge*, led the attack. One by one his squadron followed, opening fire at a hundred yards range. Frobisher's squadron followed Drake's. The Spaniards were outnumbered by about ten to one. The English had the wind behind them, and at close range their culverins made huge holes in the Spanish hulls. Spanish sails, rigging and castles were shattered. The pumps of the *San Martin* worked desperately to keep her afloat.

In the noise, smoke, and confusion it was impossible to see what was happening. Other ships gathered, but the main battle was between Drake's ships and the big galleons of the Portuguese and Seville squadrons. Three great Spanish ships sank that day, a dozen more were badly damaged. Six hundred Spaniards were killed and at least 800 wounded. The decks ran with their blood.

Toward evening after nine grueling hours, heavy rain and wind brought the battle to an end. But worse was to come. Amid the wreckage and blood and the screams of wounded men, the winds blew the helpless Spanish ships toward the treacherous sandbanks. When dawn came, the English moved in and the exhausted Spaniards prepared themselves for death. But the English were almost out of ammunition. No attack came.

Slowly the Spaniards sounded their way through the shallow waters. At any moment they might feel the terrible lurch of a ship grounded on the sands. Then in the afternoon the wind changed and blew them away from the deadly sandbanks. The Duke of Medina wrote: "We were saved by the wind, by God's mercy, it shifted to the southwest."

The English ships received little damage. Scarcely one hundred Englishmen had died since the first encounter.

Why did the great Spanish guns do so little damage? One answer may be that their cannon balls were badly cast and splintered when fired. Their gunpowder was finer ground than the English, and perhaps was unsuited to the heavy cannon. Their guns may even have exploded on their gundecks. The merchant ships were not built to take either the weight or the recoil of heavy cannon. Continual pounding from their own guns put an immense strain on the ships' timbers. Their carpenters had the never-ending task of caulking the leaks. Sometimes the guns were not properly lashed to the gundecks. When fired, the recoil sent the guns bounding across the decks, severely damaging the ships and wounding the men.

Pursuit and Confusion

After the encounter at Gravelines, Lord Howard sent frantic messages ashore for more ammunition. He did not know that the Spanish were equally short of powder and had no great shot left. Two big crippled Portuguese galleons, the *San Felipe* and the *San Mateo*, went aground on the Dutch coast, where the flyboats of Justin of Nassau, waiting like vultures, swept down and plundered them.

The Great Armada ran north before the wind that had blown it off the Flemish sandbanks. The English followed, leaving Lord Henry Seymour's squadron behind to guard the Strait of Dover. They feared the Duke of Parma would appear with his army, but he never came.

On board the *San Martin*, Medina and his advisers decided that, should the wind change, they would return to make one more attempt to link up with Parma, or attack and seize an English port. But the English held on grimly, determined to prevent the Spanish from landing on English soil. Howard followed all the way to the Firth of Forth where he gave the order to give up the chase.

Queen Elizabeth did not realize how courageously her navy had fought and grumbled that no treasure had been captured. Only

This map shows the course of the Armada as it sailed northward pursued by the English ships. Many ships never reached home. They battled with terrible weather and were sunk and wrecked around the inhospitable shores of Ireland.

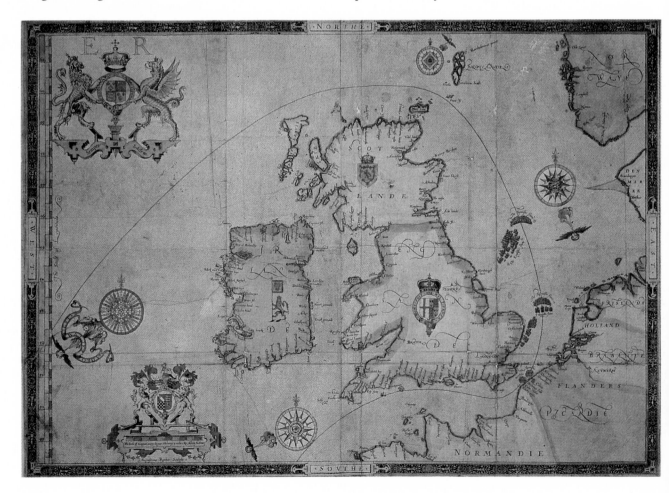

gradually did it become clear to the English that they had won a great victory and the Spanish would not return.

The End of the Armada

When the English fleet turned back, Medina and his captains held a council of war. Now their task was to get the Armada safely back to Spain. Medina wrote to the King that "the Armada was so crippled and scattered, it seemed my first duty to Your Majesty to save it, even at the risk of a very long voyage in high latitudes." The Armada was in no condition to turn back and fight its way through the Channel. Beside, the wind was still taking it north. They decided to sail around Scotland and southward in the Atlantic, keeping well away from Ireland, back to Spain.

The English, having given up the chase, sent two pinnaces to shadow the Armada as far as the Orkneys. Then they headed south. The veteran Captain Thomas Fenner of the *Non Pareil* wrote predicting the fate of the Armada. As he wrote, another terrible storm arose.

Spanish accounts of this storm describe the scattering of the fleet. But the Armada held on course. On August 19, in a moderate wind, they sailed safely through the Fair Isle channel between Shetland and the Orkneys, where Scottish fishermen sold them fish. Food was running out. Only a little slimy green water was left in the unseasoned wooden casks. Most of the biscuit, salt beef, and salt fish had gone bad. Medina had to ration the food, giving each man a daily allowance of eight ounces of biscuit, and a pint of half wine half water. Horses and mules were thrown overboard.

Of the 130 ships that had set sail from Lisbon, eight great ships had been sunk. Many pinnaces and small craft had been swept away. Half the remaining ships needed drastic repairs.

Every Spanish ship was equipped with wood for making rudders, spars for masts, oxhides and lead to patch holes, tar and oakum to caulk seams. As the Armada sailed toward Scotland, repairs were carried out. The decks of the battered ships became busy workshops as the crews tried to make them seaworthy.

Marco Aramburu, commander of *San Juan Bautista*, was helpless in the Atlantic storms. On September 15, he sighted two ships off the County Kerry coast: Recalde's *San Juan* and a frigate. The three ships managed to anchor in the calm waters of Blasket Sound. On the mainland English troops were lying in wait. After a week a storm arose and the ships began to drag their anchors. Recalde's and Aramburu's ships collided. As the sailors worked to free them the huge *Santa Maria de la Rosa* entered the Sound. She fired a gun to say she was in distress, and managed to lower one anchor. For two hours the ships struggled to maintain the anchorage. Then the *Santa Maria* dragged her cable across Aramburu's and, to the onlookers' horror, sank with all hands. The *Girona* later ran onto the rocks near the Giant's Causeway (right).

5: The Price of War

An Awful Return

Off the Orkneys, Medina sent a message to the King to say that the Armada was still together, and capable of getting back to Spain, although, besides the wounded, there were 3,000 sick on board. But soon the moderate weather changed and in the terrible seas off Cape Wrath the Armada began to break up.

In gale force winds the fleet was swept backward and forward around the north of Scotland, facing a fiercer enemy than the English: the cruel sea. The groaning, leaking ships were kept afloat by tired, hungry men working non-stop at the pumps. Scurvy, dysentery, and fever were rife. Many ships sought land, looking for food and water. Because they had abandoned their sea anchors at Calais and had only small anchors, they were often driven onto the rocks. As the weather worsened, ships were swept away from the main body of the fleet. Many sank with all hands.

Four great ships were blown back toward Shetland. The *Castello Negro* was never seen again. On September 1, the *Barca de Amburg* fired a gun to signal she was sinking. The *Gran Grifon* took off her crew, many of them wounded and dying, but was herself wrecked off Fair Isle a month later. All her 300 crew were saved, though many died afterward of hunger and fever. On September 17, the *Trinidad Valencera* struck a reef off northeast Ireland. Of the 450 men aboard, some of whom had been rescued from other ships, only 32 reached France. The rest had been slaughtered, or died of exposure or fever.

About September 18, one of the worst storms hit the Atlantic. The *Rata Santa Maria Encoronada* and the *Duquesa Santa Ana* took refuge in Blacksod Bay, County Mayo, Ireland. The *Rata* was shaken by battles and the buffetings of the storms, but worst of all, she too had lost her sea anchors. In the rising wind and tide she dragged her remaining anchor and grounded on the shelving beach. Her commander, the glamorous Don Alonso de Leyva, transferred his men to the *Santa Ana*. This was a tremendous feat, as the *Santa Ana* was anchored in another part of the bay and de Leyva had to march his men miles across a bleak headland through bogs and across rivers. The heavily laden ship set sail for Scotland, but was driven on the rocks at Loughros More in County Donegal. With great courage de Leyva, who had broken his leg, got his crew ashore. They had news that three Spanish ships were sheltering in the harbor of Killybegs. So again they set out across the mountains. At Killybegs they discovered that two of the ships were wrecked. Thirteen hundred men crammed onto the *Girona* and again set sail for Scotland. In the night the wind changed. The *Girona* hit a reef near the Giant's Causeway. Less than ten men survived; everyone else was drowned, including de Leyva who had led his men so gallantly.

In 1967 Robert Stenuit dived at the spot where local people said the *Girona* lay. He found pieces of jewelry: gold rings, bracelets, chains, crucifixes, and a tiny pendant, a beautiful salamander, the symbol of endurance. This treasure is now in the Ulster Museum, Belfast, a moving reminder of the men who met their end in such appalling circumstances.

A Famous Escape

Over a year after the defeat of the Armada a gentleman in Spain received a letter from a friend in Antwerp. The friend was Don Francisco de Cuellar, who was thought to have died in a wreck off the coast of Ireland.

When Cuellar's ship with two others had been swept into Sligo Bay, they dared not risk a landing. Ireland was wild and unruly, and English soldiers patrolled the coasts, fearing a Spanish invasion. A severe storm drove the three ships onto the beach, and over 1,000 men drowned. Cuellar grabbed a hatch cover and was swept onto the shore, smashing his leg on a timber.

Half-naked, shivering, and covered in blood, he escaped the plundering Irish and made for the woods. A beautiful girl fed him, although she took his Order of the Holy Trinity from his neck. He was helped by a priest in disguise, with whom he conversed in Latin. Then, gathering more fugitive Spaniards, he found safety in Rossclogher Castle, home of Dartry, Chief of the MacClancy clan.

The English Lord Deputy, Sir William Fitzwilliam, had raised an army of 1,700 men to exterminate the Spaniards and punish their Irish helpers. The MacClancys could not hold out against such a force, so they fled to the mountains. Cuellar and his twelve companions remained to defend the castle, armed with four boatloads of stones, six muskets, and six crossbows. The castle, set in a bog and partly surrounded by water, was difficult to attack. After seventeen days, a bitter snowstorm sent the English marching back to Dublin. The MacClancys returned and Dartry

A bucket from the wreck of the 1,100-ton Sicilian merchant ship *Trinidad Valencera*, which ran aground in Kinnagoe Bay, County Donegal in September, 1588.

offered his sister in marriage to Cuellar, begging the Spaniards to stay. But Cuellar was intent on getting home to Spain.

With four companions he left the castle secretly before dawn. He ran into some English soldiers, but once more he was rescued by women who hid him. Eventually he met a bishop who smuggled him, with other Spanish fugitives, to Scotland. A Scottish merchant took him to Flanders where the Duke of Parma was paying five ducats for each returned Spaniard. His luck held to the end. Though marauding Dutch flyboats sank his ship, he scrambled ashore at Dunkirk, one of three who survived out of 270 Spaniards who went down with his ship.

The English Aftermath

Why did the English ships stop following the Armada near the Firth of Forth? Despite the damage to the Armada at the Battle of Gravelines, only a few Spanish ships were put out of action, both fleets had run out of ammunition and the English badly needed to replenish their food and water.

On August 11, Howard, Drake, and other captains wrote to the Privy Council saying that, because food and ammunition were "in extreme scarcity," they would pursue the Armada only until it was clear of the English coast. On August 22, Howard wrote saying "the fleet is grievously infected, and men die daily." Dysentry, typhus and, some thought, plague swept the fleet.

The English ships staggered back into Harwich, Margate, Chatham, and Dover. Sir John Hawkins had hoped to organize a general discharge, but the sick were let go little by little, some with no more than a ticket to buy food for the journey home, some with only part of the money due to them. Howard beseeched the government: "Before God, I would rather have never a penny in the world, than that they should lack," and dipped into his own pocket to pay off many poor sailors.

Gradually the English realized that the Great Armada would not return. The jubilant Queen Elizabeth turned it into a personal triumph. In December 1588, she rode, like a conquering Caesar, to give thanks at St. Paul's Cathedral. Among the prayers of thanksgiving, she listened to the singing of her own composition:

"He made the winds and waters rise,
To scatter all mine Enemies."

The poor, starving, or wounded seamen and soldiers who had defeated the Armada dragged themselves home as best they could. Those who lay dying in the streets of Chatham and the east coast towns had no one to care for them. Their appalling condition prompted the compassion of Hawkins, who with Howard and Drake, began to collect sixpence a month for "poor sailors maimed in the navy."

The Aftermath

When Philip was told the dreadful news of his splendid ships, he said, "I sent them to fight against men, not storms." Regardless of cost, he set about building better ships and making more powerful arms to overcome the English.

Elizabeth's treasury was almost empty, but, with money collected from the City of London and her courtiers, she sent a fleet of 126 ships, commanded by Drake, to attack the remains of the Armada in Santander. But Drake and his captains wanted booty as well as naval victory and sailed to Corunna, hoping to attack Lisbon. Sickness broke out among the crews, and bad weather dispersed the ships. The dispirited fleet straggled back to Plymouth. The Queen was furious and Drake was in disgrace for several years.

Five years later Philip II sent 100 ships to invade England, but more than half of them were destroyed by a fierce gale in the Bay of Biscay. The following year another Spanish fleet almost reached the Lizard, but again the "winds of God" blew them back to Spain.

The "Peacemakers" confer at Somerset House in London in 1604. On the right of the window sits the Constable of Castile, leader of the Spanish Flemish delegation. On the left are the English. Second from the left is Howard of Effingham, left front is Robert Cecil, first Earl of Salisbury.

The "Armada Portrait" of Elizabeth I was painted to celebrate England's victory. Magnificently dressed, loaded with jewels, with a ruff of the most delicate lace, the Queen sits with her right hand on the globe. Behind her scenes represent victory over the Armada. She was 56 at the time, yet appears eternally young, a symbol of her power to lead her people.

In 1595, Drake, now back in favor with the Queen, set out on an expedition with Hawkins to capture treasure in the Caribbean. They were old men now by sixteenth century standards: Drake was 55, Hawkins, over 60. Near Porto Rico Hawkins fell ill and died. The Spanish were waiting with a powerful force and beat off the raiders. Drake, sad and ill with dysentery, died and was buried at sea off Puerto Bello.

In June, 1596, a magnificent fleet of 150 ships led by Howard of Effingham, Sir Walter Raleigh, and the young Earl of Essex plundered Cadiz and set fire to it. In the inner harbor the Spanish fired their own ships to prevent the English from capturing treasure worth 12,000,000 ducats. The Queen had helped fit out the fleet, and was furious with Essex for bringing back only £13,000 of booty.

Philip II of Spain died in 1598 and his son became Philip III. Still the war with England dragged on. In 1601 Spain sent her last Armada against England. A force of 500 Spanish soldiers landed at Kinsale in Ireland to help the native Irish rebellion. For three months the combined forces held out, until the more powerful English army defeated them. Sir George Carew sent the captured Spaniards home without asking for ransom. The Spanish general sent him a crate of wine and oranges to thank him for his generosity.

Peace at Last

During these disruptive years of war the English cloth trade declined. There was a boom in shipbuilding and England's forests were stripped of timber.

When Elizabeth died in 1603, James VI of Scotland became James I of England, the first Stuart monarch. He was determined to end the long war between England and Spain and in 1604 peace talks began at Somerset House in London. He started to plan a marriage for his son with the daughter of the Spanish king, just as Henry VII, the first Tudor monarch, had done over a century before. But this marriage never took place.

Index

The publishers wish to thank the following for supplying photographs for this book : 3 National Portrait Gallery London; by kind permission of the Marquess of Tavistock and the Trustees of the Bedford Estates; 6 reproduced by Gracious Permission of Her Majesty the Queen; 7 British Library; 8 top National Portrait Gallery, London; bottom National Maritime Museum, London; 11 Michael Holford; 13 top Biblioteque Nationale, Paris, bottom Rijksarchief in Zuid-Holland; 14 top National Portrait Gallery, London, bottom Collection: Plymouth City Museum and Art Gallery; 15 National Maritime Museum, London; 17 MAS, Barcelona; 18 English Heritage; 19 British Library; 20 The Huntington Library, San Marino, California; 25 Courtesy of the Marquess of Salisbury; 28 left National Maritime Museum, London, right British Library; 29 and 32 National Maritime Museum, London; 35 National Trust; 36 Ulster Museum, Belfast; 38 by kind permission of the Marquess of Tavistock and the Trustees of the Bedford Estates; 39 National Portrait Gallery, London.

DATE			